The Battle for the Cotentin Peninsula

9-19 June 1944

The Battle for the Cotentin Peninsula

9-19 June 1944

GEORGES BERNAGE

Pen & Sword
MILITARY

First published by Editions Heimdal in 2013 as *La Bataille du Cotentin: 9-19 juin 1944*

First published in Great Britain in 2018 by
Pen & Sword Military
An imprint of
Pen & Sword Books Ltd
47 Church Street
Barnsley
South Yorkshire
S70 2AS

Copyright © Georges Bernage, 2018

ISBN 978 1 47385 763 6

The right of Georges Bernage to be identified as Author of this work has been asserted by him in accordance with the Copyright, Designs and Patents Act 1988.

A CIP catalogue record for this book is
available from the British Library.

Typeset by Aura Technology and Software Services, India
Printed and bound in India
By Replika Press Pvt Ltd.

Pen & Sword Books Ltd incorporates the Imprints of Pen & Sword Books Archaeology, Atlas, Aviation, Battleground, Discovery, Family History, History, Maritime, Military, Naval, Politics, Railways, Select, Transport, True Crime, Fiction, Frontline Books, Leo Cooper, Praetorian Press, Seaforth Publishing, Wharncliffe and White Owl.

For a complete list of Pen & Sword titles please contact
PEN & SWORD BOOKS LIMITED
47 Church Street, Barnsley, South Yorkshire, S70 2AS, England
E-mail: enquiries@pen-and-sword.co.uk
Website: www.pen-and-sword.co.uk

Contents

1

Advancing from the Bridgehead

By 13 June 1944, it had been a week since the Allies had landed in Normandy. One week. What is a week in peacetime? Hardly anything. However, for those soldiers engaged in the fighting through the Normandy *bocage*, every hour is an eternity. Every minute can be the one where you meet an enemy bullet, or a fatal shell burst. Just a few minutes under artillery fire or bombardment can constitute an infernal ordeal, and already in these few days, thousands of soldiers had been killed or wounded. After this first week of the Battle of Normandy, the bridgehead was very wide, but still shallow, having only advanced 10-20 kilometres inland; very little when one considers that the Allied divisions were completely motorised, involving thousands of vehicles, enormous reserves of equipment and fuel, and ammunition piled up in enclosures. Moving from the coast to the front line would take a good walker only one to two hours, passing camps and stockpiles of resources along the way. A cloud of dust and exhaust fumes hung over this coastal fringe of the Normandy landscape. In addition, in the midst of this mass advanced airfields still occupied precious hectares of land. The Allies had the support of their fleet, which was able to crush German counter-attacks with the heavy guns of the naval artillery. They also had at their disposal their advanced airfields, from which the Tactical Air Forces planes attacked and destroyed

This bronze statue of an American parachutist looks out over the Merderet Valley and the La Fière Memorial Park. The initial attempt to cross the causeway on 6 June, and then the successful crossing on 9 June, was a memorable moment for the US Army, similar to that of the Battle d'Arcole for the French, or Agincourt for the English. The site, situated north of the causeway access, is now well-established and signposted from Sainte-Mère-Eglise. (E.Groult/Heimdal)

the columns of German vehicles. However, in addition to these two weapons that could crush the German front, in order to win the Allies needed numerical superiority for their troops on the ground, and at present, they dramatically lacked the space needed to bring across other divisions as reinforcements.

In this context, the Cotentin Peninsula constituted a large area of ground approximately 40 kilometres long and 40 kilometres wide. In addition, at the end of the peninsula was the large transatlantic port of Cherbourg. The peninsula itself would be able to serve as a base for gathering several divisions, as well as having a major port that was essential to the Allies for receiving supplies. The conquest of the Cotentin Peninsula was now a priority objective, and the Battle of Cherbourg would begin.

Shoulder badge of the 82nd Airborne Division.

Four days earlier, on 9 June, VII Corps (under the command of General Collins), was ordered to take the Cotentin Peninsula and march towards Cherbourg. It was currently holding the bridgehead from Utah Beach, which was still dramatically 'boxed in', and once more, the 82nd Airborne Division would be put into action.

American Paratroopers on the Front Line

Following the heavy fighting by the airborne troops from 6 to 8 June, the 82nd Airborne Division would remain on the front line for the breakthrough beyond the Merderet River. It was commanded by Major General Mathew B. Ridgway, who was born on 3 March 1895 in Fort Monroe, Virginia. He graduated from West Point in 1917 and was posted overseas (China, Philippines, Nicaragua), but also to West Point and Fort Benning. He attended the U.S. Army Command and General Staff School, then held various staff positions before taking command of the 82nd Airborne Division in June 1942. He was assisted by Brigadier General James M. Gavin, who was second-in-command of the division. Gavin was born in Brooklyn on 22 March 1907, and joined the army aged seventeen, later attending West Point. In 1929 he served as a second lieutenant in the infantry, then as an instructor at West Point, before joining the 503rd Parachute Infantry Battalion in September 1941. He attended classes at the U.S. Army Command and General Staff School in February 1942, before taking command of the 505th Parachute Infantry Regiment six months later. In February 1944 he became the second-in-command

1. Major General Ridgway, commander of the 82nd Airborne Division.

2. Brigadier General James M. Gavin, the division's second-in-command.

of the 82nd Airborne Division, which he assumed commanded of in August 1944 after replacing Major General Ridgway (who would assume command of the XVIII Airborne Corps). At only 38-years-old, Gavin had become the youngest major general in the United States Army.

The 82nd Airborne Division comprised of three parachute infantry regiments (PIR): the 505th, 507th, and 508th, as well as the 325th Glider Infantry Regiment (GIR). The division also had an airborne artillery group (456th Parachute Field Artillery Battalion), two field artillery groups (319th and 320th Glider Field Artillery Battalions), and an anti-aircraft group (80th Anti-aircraft Battalion).

1. Panoramic view of the Merderet Valley from the north of the La Fière Causeway. On the left can be seen the buildings below the manor house, the road, and then Cauquigny, which can be seen in the background behind the trees. 'Timmes' Orchard' was on the right, in front of Amfreville. It was via this 'hidden road' or 'secret ford', seen just to the right, which allowed the 1/325 to cross the flooded valley. This photograph was taken on the eastern shore, where the statue of the paratrooper dominates the memorial park. Like others in this chapter, this image was taken during the winter, after a very rainy season, so the water level is similar to what it would have been in June 1944. (E. Groult/Heimdal)

2. Looking from the road, the 'Gray Castle' can be seen behind the trees. The marshland is behind the chateau. (G. Bernage)

Amfreville and the memorial plaque placed at the entrance of the road leading to the chateau, the 'Gray Castle', where the Germans of II./1057 were in position. (G. Bernage)

Cette maison, réquisitionnée par l'occupant, était utilisée pour y détenir et interroger les prisonniers en juin 1944.

Le lieutenant américain **Walter "Chris" Heisler,** du 507ᵉᵐᵉ P.I.R., était l'un d'entre eux.

1. Lieutenant John Marr (G Company, 507th PIR) was sent by Lieutenant Colonel Timmes to establish a link with the 1/325 (Sanford) on the eastern bank. He discovered the 'secret ford' and accomplished his mission; bringing back the 1/325 to the western bank.

2. Colonel G.V. Millett commanded the 507th PIR, elements of whom were isolated west of Amfreville. His mission was to rejoin Timmes during the night of 8-9 June, but he failed and was taken prisoner.

3. Lieutenant Charles G. Timmes (2/507) commanded a hundred or so men who had been trapped in an orchard (Timmes' Orchard), east of Amfreville, on the western bank of the Merderet, since 6 June. The operation during the night of 8-9 was intended to rescue them.

4. Private First Class Charles N. DeGlopper, C Company, 1/325, who sacrificed himself by providing covering fire with his BAR machine gun as his comrades fell into an ambush at 04:30 on 9 June. He protected their retreat and posthumously received the Congressional Medal of Honor.

to attack from the east. He planned to take the road under German fire, and engage Lieutenant Colonel Carrell's 3rd Battalion, the 3/325. The attack would be launched with the support of covering fire by the paratroopers from Captain Rae's company, who would be in position along the shore. The artillery began its preparation at 10 am on 9 June. Three days earlier, on 6 June, a first attack had failed after it was pushed back by the French Renault tanks used by the Panzer-Ersatz-und-Ausbildungs-Abteilung 100. Three of the tanks had been destroyed by bazookas, and their wreckages now lay on the roadway as a testimony of this first battle.

Colonel Lewis, who commanded the regiment, then ordered Lieutenant Colonel Charles Carrell, an officer from West Point Military Academy, to cross the roadway and set up a bridgehead on the other side. Lewis then asked Lieutenant Vernon Wyant, the liaison officer, to bring him Brigadier General Gavin's report. According to Wyant, Carrell considered the attack on the road to be a 'suicide mission' and showed no compassion for him. Carrell had, in fact, been wounded when his glider landed and showed little enthusiasm for this new attack. Meanwhile, Gavin, who was unacquainted with this depressed officer, gave an 'emphatic' direct order to launch the attack at once. According

1. One of the three Renault tanks used by the Germans and destroyed on 6 June 1944. (US Army)

2. The location of Brigadier James Gavin's command post near the manor house at la Fière and the access to the causeway, on the south side of the road. (G. Bernage)

3. The manor house at La Fière with its round tower, typical of the sixteenth century. (G. Bernage)

1. Panoramic view of the La Fière Causeway and the flooded valley of the Merderet. The hamlet of Cauquigny was 450 metres away. Here, the winter rains have raised the water levels to what they would have been in June 1944. (E. Groult/Heimdal)

2. Captain Robert Rae in July 1944 at the Broquebeuf manor house, near Lithaire, where he received the DSC following his actions at La Fière. (D.F. Heimdal)

3. The causeway is flanked by embankments in the last 100 metres before the hamlet of Cauquigny, which can be seen in the background. By this time, they were encumbered with dead and wounded. (G. Bernage.)

to Clay Blair (in his book, *Ridgway's Paratroopers*), Gavin quickly shouted, 'Let's go! Let's go!' But Carrell replied: 'I don't think I can do it!' When Gavin asked why not, Carrell replied that he was 'sick'. The latter then gathered his company commanders and gave his orders: Captain John Sauls and G Company would take the lead, followed by E Company and then Captain Harvey with F Company. However, the outcome of the battle had depended on the rapidity of

the attack, and Colonel Lewis consequently relieved Carrell of his command and replaced him immediately with Major General Arthur Gardner, a regimental staff officer. However, according to Wayne Pierce (in his book, *Let's Go*), the men of the battalion did not know this officer, and instead preferred Major Charles Moore following his conduct during the attack. Companies G, E and F would have to charge along the causeway to the chapel at Cauquigny.

At 10:30, the artillery of the 90th Infantry Division opened fire as the battalion, which was at Chef-du-Pont, arrived at la Fière, at the top of the causeway at 10:45. Lieutenant Colonel Frank Norris' 105 mm guns provided a smoke screen to cover the attack, and as a cloud of black smoke spread out over Cauquigny, the German fired their own guns in response. Sherman tanks from the 746th Tank Battalion, who were positioned near the manor house at la Fière, 100-150 metres from the bridge, also provided covering fire for Captain Sauls' men, as he rushed to the head of G Company, followed by Lieutenant Donald B. Wason, Sergeant Wilfred Ericsson, and the rest of the company. One of the accompanying tanks landed on an American mine, and unfortunately, running for 450 metres under automatic fire and mortar shells proved too much. Lieutenant Donald Wason was killed and many of the men crawled into the ditches along the causeway.

Captain Sauls and Sergeant Ericsson were now on the other side, but the destroyed American tank, as well as the three German tanks, created a bottleneck which slowed the flow of men towards the west. Another platoon arrived on the other side, and German prisoners who had been flushed out along the banks were now sent back to the manor house. The losses, however, had been heavy.

Lieutenant Richard B. Johnson now rushed to the head of E Company. Having begun with 148 men when they set off from the manor house at la Fière, the company could already count 35 dead along the causeway. The company commander, Captain Charles F. Murphy, was wounded in the face and now lay at the side of the road, surrounded by four of his men who had been killed by mortar bursts. The company had been deployed on the right, attacking Cauquigny, aiming to clear the ground to the north and around the chapel. Sergeant Frank Studant collapsed as he arrived near the chapel, after being struck in the heart by a bullet. Lieutenant Bruce H. Booker was injured after his legs were blown away, but he managed to climb onto the embankment and urge his men to keep advancing. His section would capture German soldiers and a mortar team as they arrived at the chapel, although the Germans were also encouraged to surrender after coming under fire from Captain Rae's men on the other shore.

Captain James M. Harney then arrived at the head of F Company, while the tanks located near the manor house continued to fire on Cauquigny. Owing to

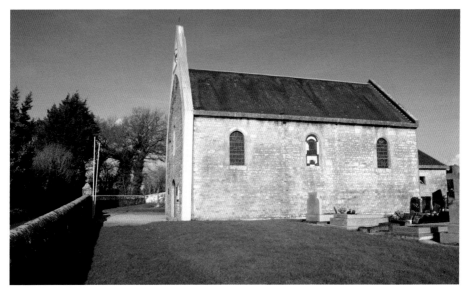

The hamlet of Cauquigny, located at the end of the La Fière Causeway, was an important objective on 9 June, after the failure of the operation on the previous night. The destruction from the fighting can be seen here, showing the chapel at the time and in 2013, after being restored. The chapel has also become a memorial to the 82nd Airborne Division, including a display panel (as at La Fière), describing the actions that took place there. (Amfreville OT and E.G./Heimdal)

One of the photographs on the display panel, showing privates Levy and Korilo in front of the chapel. (Amfreville OT)

the small size of the bridgehead, it continued to extend towards the west and the three companies were distributed as follows from north to south: F, E and G (see map).

On the eastern shore, the progress made by the 3/325 was misunderstood, and believing that the battalion had failed in its attack, Brigadier General Gavin ordered Captain Robert D. Rae to cross the road with his paratroopers from the 507 PIR. Rae picked up the stragglers from the other companies and advanced at about the same time as F Company, moving alongside together. Rae joined forces with Captain Harney and advanced to the edge of the hamlet of Motey, although Harney remained at the captured chapel at Cauquigny, while Captain Sauls returned to la Fière and brought back two Sherman tanks. Harney then sent a platoon to the north to establish contact with the Timmes, while F Company remained along the main road. Tanks from the 746th Battalion arrived around noon, missing the end of the battle. At Motey, the arriving troops mistakenly came under fire from the American artillery and had to fall back. Captain Rae returned to Cauquigny and sent a patrol to Timmes' battalion; contact was made, meaning the battalion was now connected to the bridgehead. The northern flank was assured.

However, the discovery of German soldiers behind a hedge forced Harney to back off a little, as panic began to emerge in this fragile bridgehead, before it was stabilised by the arrival of reinforcements as E Company was brought back into

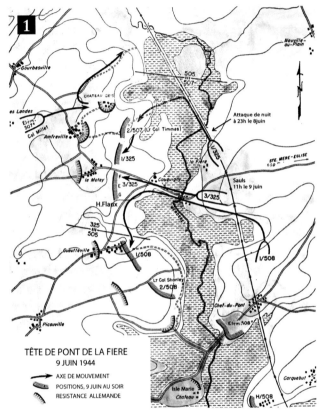

1. Map showing the Meredet Valley and the operations on the night of 8-9 June 1944 and the following day. (Heimdal, after a US Army map)

2. American aerial photograph from 1944 taken in the direction of the attack, looking westward, from La Fière. The hamlet of Cauquigny can be seen on the other side, the fork in the road, then the hamlet of Motey. Amfreville is on the right, as well as le Hameau aux Brix. Le Hameau Flaux is on the left. The water has been coloured in. (Heimdal)

line. Positions were finally established in the late afternoon and communications were even established with the Shanley Group, further south. Thus, the bridgehead was now continuous, encompassing the Timmes Group in the north and the Shanley Group in the south. Reinforcements from the 90th Infantry Division would arrive the following day in order to continue the offensive towards the west.

This attack along the la Fière Causeway would become an epic tale in the history of the US Army, and could be regarded as their 'Agincourt'.

90th Division Move to the Front

For the offensive on the Cotentin Peninsula, VII Corps had planned to place the 90th Infantry Division to the right of the 4th Infantry Division. The division had been formed in August 1917 at the Travis Center, Texas, and was made up of men from Texas and Oklahoma, hence its emblem of the interlaced initials of the two states, and its nickname, "Texas Oklahoma Division". The initials would also give rise to another nickname for the troupe: "Tough 'Ombres" (tough guys), and the motto: "Here comes the ninetieth again". In the First World War the division had arrived in France in June and July 1918, to relieve the 1st Infantry Division in August, and in September it was engaged in the offensive at Saint-Mihiel, and the Meuse-Argonne offensive in October. It would contribute to the breakthrough of the Hindenburg Line, taking 1,876 prisoners but losing 7,277 men in the process. It returned to the USA in June 1919 following period of occupation in Germany, and was disbanded shortly thereafter.

Looking south down the flooded Meredet Valley from the La Fière Causeway, towards the other road from Chef-du-Pont (left) to Beuzeville-la-Bastille (right). In the middle stands Marie Island and its castle, flanked by round towers, where a group of Germans still held their position. (G. Bernage)

1. Fabric shoulder badge showing the emblem of the 90th Infantry Division.

2. The interlocking initials 'TO' (standing for Texas Oklahoma) were painted in red on the soldiers' helmets. (Private collection)

The division was reconstituted on 25 March 1942 at Camp Barkeley, Texas, and participated in major manoeuvres in Louisiana in February and March 1943. In September the men underwent training in the desert before being transferred to Fort Dix, New Jersey, and leaving the USA in March 1944. Once in England, it took part in amphibious training. The division was made up of three infantry regiments; (the 357th, 358th and 359th Infantry Regiments), and artillery groups, (the 343rd, 344th, 915th (L) and 345th (M) Field Artillery Battalions).

The first elements of the division landed at Utah Beach on 6 June with the 4th Infantry Division, with the remainder of the unit following on 7 and 8 June. By 10 June, the division was fully assembled, under the command of General Jay W. McKelvie and received its first mission; it was ordered to cross the Merderet, behind the 82nd Airborne Division, to try and penetrate to the west of this flooded valley, towards Picauville. This meant a change of direction; they would no longer

Helmet belonging to Lieutenant Colonel John B. Daly, from San Francisco, who was killed on 19 August 1944 in Chambois. It bears the emblem of the 90th Infantry Division (in red paint) and his grade badge. (Private collection)

advance to the north, but to the west. Indeed, on 9 June, after the 4th Infantry Division's failure in the Montebourg area, General Bradley was unable to take the direct route to Cherbourg, and so decided to push west in order to cut off the Cotentin Peninsula. Consequently, on 9 June, General MacKelvie received verbal orders to rejoin the Merderet bridgehead.

General Hellmich at Malassis

The western part of the peninsula was defended by the 243. Infanterie Division, a unit that had been formed in Döllersheim, in July 1943, and sent to Normandy in the autumn of that same year. The plan was to turn this static division into a battlefield unit, and by 1 May 1944 it had 11,529 men, making it one of the most powerful in the West at that time. It was made up of three infantry regiments (Gren.-Regt. 920, 921 and 922), with three battalions in each, except for the GR 920, which only had two. The GR 920 (commanded by Colonel Klosterkemperer) was based in la Hague before the invasion. GR921 (Lieutenant Colonel Simon) was based in the Barneville area, with its CP at the Hotel Mauger, near Saint-Maurice-en-Cotentin. Meanwhile, the GR 922 (Lieutenant Colonel Müller) was in the Pieux sector. Each regiment had a company of infantry artillery (the 13.IG Kompanie) each comprising six Russian 7.62 cm howitzers. The 14. Pak-Kompanie of each of the regiments included three 7.5 cm anti-tank guns. With the exception of those in the GR 920 (who travelled on foot and by horse-drawn cart), all of the infantry companies (Grenadieren) travelled by bicycle.

The artillery regiment, Artillerie-Regiment 243 (whose CP was at Vrétot, near the division's headquarters), had Russian 7.62 cm guns (four per battery) for its first two groups (three batteries each) and for the third group, (III./243), 12.2 cm Russian howitzers for the 7th to 9th batteries, and four Russian 12.2 cm guns for the 10th Battery. All of the batteries were motorised, which was a step forward in the division's evolution towards greater mobility. It also had armoured vehicles, including the Panzerjäger-Abteilung 243 (group of tank hunters), who were equipped with Marder 38s and Sturmgeschütz IIIs, and who joined the division in March 1944.

The division was commanded by Generalleutnant Heinz Hellmich. Born on 9 June 1890 in Karlsruhe, near the banks of the Rhine, Hellmich became a 'Kadet' in the Imperial Army in 1908 and was assigned to 122. Infanterie-Regiment as a Leutnant on 22 March 1910. He fought during the First World War and afterwards remained in the army, now reduced to 100,000 men, where he was still serving in 1933 when Hitler came to power. A very professional and highly competent officer, Hellmich rapidly climbed the ladder and was promoted to lieutenant colonel in 1934, colonel in 1936 and Generalmajor in 1939, as a member of the General Staff attached to the Luftwaffe. At the beginning of the war he was chief of staff of Heeresgruppe B in October 1939. He was noticed for his talents and on 1 June 1940, was given command of the 23. Infanterie-Division. The division was sent to East Prussia in September 1940, and on 22 June 1941, took part in Operation Barbarossa (the invasion of the Soviet Union), seeing action in battles of Bialystok, Minsk and Smolensk, right up to the gates of Moscow in December 1941. Hellmich was promoted to Generalleutnant on 1 September 1940, but the division suffered enormously during the winter campaign, and had only three infantry battalions in

January 1942. There was no artillery, the horses having died because of the intense cold. The general's nerves cracked and he was sent to Germany on 17 January 1942, marking the end of a very promising career.

On 1 April 1942, Hellmich was assigned to a mobilisation centre in Insterburg, East Prussia, which testifies to his decline. However, on 15 December 1942 he was appointed inspector of the Osttruppen ("Eastern Troops") and became General der Osttruppen, which involved overseeing the training of Soviet volunteers (prisoners of war or Russian volunteers, or national minorities with autonomist attitudes). As the Germans began to retreat, the mission lost its importance and on 10 January 1944, Hellmich obtained a new command at the head of a fighting unit, arriving in the Cotentin Peninsula and becoming Kommandeur of the 243. Infanterie-Division. He also came across soldiers he knew well, the Osttruppen, and in particular Ost-Battalion 561 (in position in the Cap de Flamanville area, which would serve as 3rd Battalion for GR 920) and Ost-Battalion 795, (primarily Georgians), who after being stationed in la Hague, would join the Turqueville sector, south of Sainte-Mère-Eglise, before 6 June 1944.

General Heinz Hellmich, commander of 243. Infanterie-Division inspecting Ost-Battalion 795 on the north-west coast of the Cotentin Peninsula (at the hamlet of Asselins at Digulleville) in La Hague, before the battalion of Georgian volunteers was transferred to the east coast, south of Sainte-Mère-Eglise, on 14 May 1944. The general was an 'Eastern Troops' specialist and is seen here examining a machine-gun of Soviet origin, a 7.62 mm MG 216 (r), manufactured from 1940-1943. (BHVP)

1. General Heinz Hellmich at his desk. (J. Charita)

2. The former command post of General Hellmich, at Malassis. Arriving by the road from le Vrétot, one first passes in front of the chateau, a large nineteenth-century house which had been transformed for agricultural use. (J. Bavay)

1. The old manor buildings had been turned into a farm, forming a square courtyard. This building on the left, with its arched doorways and chamfered windows, dates from the sixteenth century, but is now used as a barn. (E.G./Heimdal)

2. The courtyard before the war, as General Hellmich and his staff would have known it. The small building on the left, with its round tower, is also from the sixteenth century. The main house in the background is slightly later, dating from the beginning of the seventeenth century. Its triangular pediments above the windows and a mullion window on the ground floor, has since disappeared. The general slept in this house. The small sixteenth-century house is behind the photographer and the building that was used as a cinema was presumably located on the right. (Delacour/Heimdal)

General Hellmich's headquarters were at the chateau and manor house at Malassis, south of le Vrétot (south-west of Bricquebec). It was actually located between Le Vrétot and Les Perques, south-east of Vrétot, on the side of a valley overlooking La Scye, and was made up of sixteenth and seventeenth-century buildings that surrounded a square courtyard, while slightly below was a large nineteenth-century house that was called the 'chateau'. These buildings, mainly for agricultural use, were acquired in 1933 by Monsieur Leroy.

Blanche Delacour (née Leroy), is one of his daughters. Now 83-years-old, she describes how the place looked when it served as headquarters for the 243. Infanterie-Division:

The farm was occupied by the Germans. There were barracks everywhere, in the driveway leading to the farm and under the oaks (which have disappeared today). They had put the horses in the stables; our cows were in the meadows. One day, a German who was in the farmyard told me, 'I have a daughter about your age in Germany'. I was fifteen. There were seven [of us] children, five girls and two boys. Papa did not want us to go up to the chateau.

On the evening of Monday, 5 June, my mother was coming back from milking, but was still in the garden. My father had gone to Caen to get some string. I had locked the cellar. The Germans were in the cinema (a farm building that had become a gaming room and where they played films). I often saw the Vicomtesse [Viscountess] de Plinval there when she came. A German soldier stood guard in the courtyard. A young man came to tell us that our father was most likely not coming back that night because the railway tracks had been bombed. My sister, Eugénie, was still in the dairy. All of a sudden the bombs fell. The young man took my little brother, opened the gate and went to hide. The horses were frightened and agitated. The soldier in the yard told my sister to come and see the sky. She said, 'I'm coming, but I need to stop the separator'. When she came out, the soldier was dead. He was the only victim. You couldn't see anything in the yard because there was so much smoke. Fortunately, several of the bombs didn't explode (just behind the house, under the bakery...) otherwise there would have been more fatalities. The butter was full of shrapnel and a pig had been hit by a splinter, but wasn't dead. The general told Mother, 'Gather your children and hide. There were no fatalities'. She replied, 'Yes, and that one?' showing him the body. We put some clothes together and left. When we came back, the Germans had all gone. (Testimony collected by Jeannine Bavay)

The Viscomtesse de Plinval denounced many of the region's inhabitants to the Germans, and after the war was condemned to death. Blanche Delacour also recalls that General Hellmich spoke good French.

This bombardment, which took place during the night of 5-6 June, was obviously aimed at the division's headquarters, but probably also Artillery-Regiment 243, which was located at Vrétot. According to Blanche Delacour, other bombs fell further north that night, which matches the testimony of Charles Montrieul, who was 9-years-old at the time and was the son of Vrétot's mayor:

A stick of bombs fell on the top of the Vrétot hills (500 metres, as the crow files, from Malassis). Madame Gallien's house, the closest to the Carteret road, was hit, and Madame Gallien herself was killed as she had been standing in front of the door. A bomb fell upstream of the Boisselerie bridge on the road to Carteret, but it did not explode.

1. Today, the mullion and dormer windows have disappeared. Part of the building on the left, between the turret and the house, was damaged by the bombardment of 5 June 1944 and then rebuilt after the war. (E.G./Heimdal)

2. The farm building where the Germans set up their common room, which included a cinema. (E.G/Heimdal)

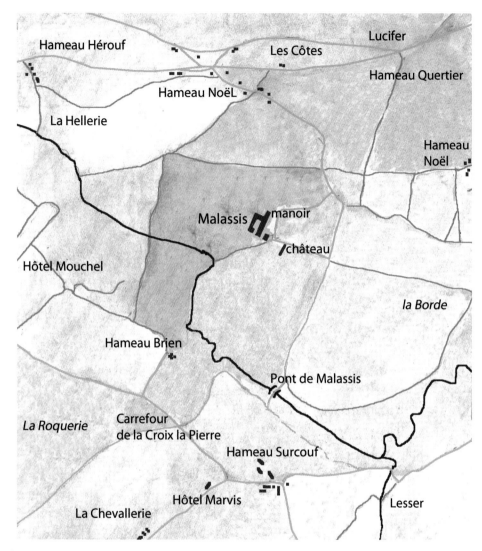

Hameau Hérouf

Lucifer

Les Côtes

Hameau Quertier

Hameau NoëL

La Hellerie

Hameau
Noël

Malassis   manoir

château

Hôtel Mouchel

la Borde

Hameau Brien

Pont de Malassis

La Roquerie

Carrefour
de la Croix la Pierre

Hameau Surcouf

Hôtel Marvis

Lesser

La Chevallerie

General Hellmich's command post was located at Malassis, in the Vrétot commune, south of the Bricquebec-Carteret road, halfway up a valley and overlooking the Scye. One had to pass in front of the chateau in order to arrive at the manor-farm. (E.G./Heimdal)

And so the bombardment that was intended for General Hellmich had, in fact, only killed one German soldier and an unfortunate civilian.

The Ivy Division head for Montebourg

The 4th Infantry Division landed at Utah Beach on 6 June 1944. It was commanded by Major General Raymond O. Barton, who was born on 22 August 1889 in Granada, Colorado, the son of Conway O. Barton and Carrie Mosher. He left West Point in 1912 and, as a second lieutenant, was assigned to the 30th Infantry Regiment in Alaska. He was an instructor from 1917-18 and, promoted to captain, went to France in August 1919 where he served in the

General Barton, commander of
4th Infantry Division.

8th Infantry Regiment. He returned to the USA with this regiment with the rank of major. While awaiting a new command, he was admitted to the General Staff School, at Fort Leavenworth, Kansas, and then to the Army War College in Washington. He served as deputy chief of staff for VII Corps from 1924 to 1928. Promoted to lieutenant colonel in 1935, he returned to the 8th Infantry Regiment, assuming command from the end of 1938 to July 1940, when he became chief of staff for 4th Infantry Division. Promoted to brigadier general then major general in 1942, he took command of 4th Infantry Division in June 1942. He began to prepare the division for the mission that would be his two years later. Barton was noted as a good leader of men, knowing how to prepare his unit carefully for a mission. He led several amphibious manoeuvres at Camp Gordon Johnston, in Florida, and shortly before the D-Day landings at Slapton Sands, in the south of England. He remained in command of the division until the end of December 1944, before being posted to the infantry training centre at Fort McCellan, USA, in March 1945. He left the army in 1946 died on 27 February 1963 at Fort Gordon, Georgia.

The 4th Infantry Division was set up at Greene Camp in 1917 under the command of Major General George H. Cameron, and landed in France on 5 June 1918. On the voyage over, the ship carrying it, the *Maldovia*, was torpedoed by a German submarine, resulting in the loss of fifty-six men. The division would take part in the Aisne-Meuse, Saint-Mihiel and Meuse-Argonne offensives, and would remain in Germany for six months after the war, before being repatriated to the USA and disbanded. It was finally restored on 1 June 1940 at Fort Benning, Georgia, where it began its training. It then moved to Camp Gordon, Georgia, and passed under the command of the 2nd Army. In April 1943, it left the south for Fort Dix, New Jersey, where it continued training under General Barton until September, before returning to Camp Johnston, Florida, for amphibious exercises. In December, it moved to Fort Jackson, South Carolina, and embarked for Great Britain in January 1944, continuing its training in Devon and participating in further amphibious exercises at Slapton Sands.

This division was called the Ivy Division due to its insignia of four ivy leaves arranged in a cross, facing north, south, east and west, with the stems emerging from a circle. These leaves also evoke the division's number, and the pronunciation of the word i-vy suggests the Roman numeral IV. It was comprised

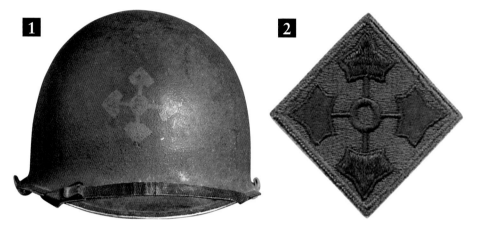

1. Helmet showing the emblem of 4th Division. (Private collection)

2. Fabric badge worn on the top of the left shoulder by the men of 4th Infantry Division, the Ivy Division, showing its ivy leaves.

of three infantry regiments: the 8th (Colonel James A. Van Fleet), 12th (Colonel Russell P. ("Red") Reeder) and 22nd (Colonel Hervery A. Tribolet) Infantry Regiments, and four artillery groups: the 29th, 42nd and 44th Self-Propelled (L) Field Artillery Battalions (light self-propelled groups), as well as the 20th Field Artillery Battalion.

General Omar Bradley regarded this 18,000-strong division as 'superbly trained' (it was true in the sense that its training had lasted four years...), and was thus chosen to land at Utah Beach. Faced with a weak opposition, the landing was a success, resulting in few losses (197 men, of which 60 were lost at sea). It established the junction with the airborne troops at the exit of beaches, before heading north. On 9 June it advanced 4.8 kilometres (3 miles) in that direction towards its objective, Cherbourg. However it would be halted at Montebourg and would undergo three days of very hard fighting.

The *Kampfgruppe* Keil

On 6 June the Cotentin Peninsula was defended by three static infantry divisions: the 709. Infanterie-Division (Generalleutnant Karl Wilhelm von Schlieben) to the east, from Val de Saire and Cherbourg to Baie des Veys; the 243. Infanterie-Division (Generalleutnant Heinz Hellmich) and the 91. (LL) Infanterie-Division (Generalmajor Wilhelm Falley), in the centre of the peninsula. This division had arrived shortly before the invasion and had forced the Allies to modify their plans for airborne operations (see G. Bernage, *Objectif Carentan*, Heimdal). However this last division had been decapitated; Generalmajor Falley having been killed by American paratroopers from the Schegel Group on the night of 5-6 June as he was returning to his CP at the Bernaville chateau, in Picauville (see Utah Beach, Heimdal, pp. 89-92). Following the shock of these first operations, the 91st and 709th divisions had already incurred substantial losses.

Facing General Barton's 4th Infantry Division were mainly elements of the 709. Infanterie-Division, especially one of its regiments; Grenadier-Regiment 919 (raised in Hesse and Thuringia) and commanded by Oberstleutnant Günther Keil. The regiment was mainly made up of older recruits, with 75 per cent of its non-commissioned officers and men being between thirty-five and forty-five years of age. On the other hand, 25 per cent of them were veterans of the Eastern Front and, despite being old, had good military experience. The commander of the regiment and his battalion commanders were experienced officers, as they would brilliantly prove, while the rest were reserve officers with no military experience. However, half of the company commanders were former active NCOs with good military training, but by the end of 1944, some of the younger soldiers had joined the Eastern Front and were then replaced by even younger soldiers (18-19-years-old) with no military experience.

As a result, while the 82nd Airborne Division was fighting to set foot on the west bank of the Merderet, north of the bridgehead, the German Front held firm and blocked the RN13 road; the direct route to Cherbourg. The large village of Montebourg lays along this road, positioned up on an eminence that dominates the entire area, with the Gothic spires of the church rising up and providing a point of reference that is visible from some distance away. In the village, on the north-south axis of the RN13, is the vast rectangular market square, where the feast of Candlemas takes place in February. Parallel to the square, to the east, is another smaller square containing the Gothic church. To the south-east of the vicinity, the old abbey forms a sort of bastion, built

View of the marshes looking towards Beauzeville la Bastille. (E.G./Heimdal)

behind the high walls from which a powerful, medieval fortified gate opens. American paratroopers were in Sainte-Mère-Eglise, a town 10 kilometres south of Montebourg, from the night of 5-6 June. As early as 8 June, GIs from the 4th Infantry Division had already taken Emondeville and Azeville (but not the perimeter of the German battery, which was still in enemy hands), less than 3 kilometres from Montebourg.

On the German side, Generalleutnant Keil's Grenadier-Regiment 919 would form the defensive pivot in the Montebourg sector. As we have seen, the attack by the 12th US Infantry Regiment nearly reached Montebourg on 8 June. On the night of 8-9 June, the Panzer-Ersatz-Abteilung 100, a battalion equipped with twenty-five light French tanks under the command of Hauptmann Wenk, took up its position to defend the village, after having lost several tanks on the la Fière Causeway. This battalion thus came under the Keil's command. On 9 June, III./919 arrived from the south-east to strengthen the area's defence to the east and south-east. The same day, 9./919 (one of the battalion's four companies) was removed and was reattached to II./920, another battalion that was holding the front line further east, in the area around Saint-Floxel. Command of the Montebourg sector was entrusted to Hauptmann Simoneit, who had been named Kampfkommandant on 7 June. Simoneit was in direct radio contact with General von Schlieben and depended on his staff. This grouping of various forces gathered together for a specific, tactical occasion is called a *Kampfgruppe* by the German Army, who would make much use of this very effective system, which was adopted by the US military under the name 'Combat Command'. The battle group formed under the authority of Oberstleutnant Keil took the name of *Kampfgruppe* Keil, and would gain renown for its defence of Montebourg.

2

Difficult Progress: 10-13 June

Saturday 10 June

The 90th Infantry Division's mission was to cross at La Fière and Chef-du-Pont and then attack west from these crossing points. Its first objective was the Douve Valley, from Saint-Sauveur-le-Vicomte to la Terre de Beauval, north of the valley. From there, it would go north towards Cherbourg, on the left flank of the 4th Division; note that for the time being, it was not a matter of 'cutting off' of the peninsula, but of widening the bridgehead in the west in order to advance north towards Cherbourg. However, destiny would alter these plans twice over. As Major Ruppenthal noted, 'The 82nd Airborne Division would hold the lines of the Merderet until the 90th Division had advanced around 1.8 km west of the river, before supporting the southern flank of VII Corps on the northern banks of the Douve.'

At the beginning of the operation, General McKelvie only had two infantry regiments, as the 359th IR was still under the authority of 4th Division.

In the early hours of 10 June, the 357th IR advanced along the causeway towards Amfreville, before continuing on to Orglandes and Sainte-Colombe. At 04:00 it came under German fire and suffered some casualties, as well as a delay in the advance. Fortunately, the 325th GIR provided protection on the bridgehead, where the Germans from GR 1057 (it was in fact its 2nd Battalion, II./1057, 91st (LL) Infantry Division, which was in position in the Picauville sector on 6 June), held their strong positions and exerted pressure [on the Americans]. But what was a single German battalion compared to all these American units? Nevertheless, it was a baptism of fire for the 357th IR, who lost ground and had to re-gather in the positions of the 325th GIR. In this desperate situation, 2./357 arrived at 21:30 to relieve 1./357. This new battalion launched an attack on Amfreville, but it was a failure and the regiment suffered heavily: fifteen dead and eighty-one wounded, meaning ninety-nine casualties in total.

To the south, protected by Colonel Shanley, who held Hill 30, to the north of the causeway, the 358th IR launched its 1st Battalion, 1/358, from Chef-du Pont. It managed to cross the causeway by 05:30 and was then followed by 3rd Battalion. Its opposition: a few rifle shots fired from the chateau on the Isle-Marie, located to the south of the causeway, and so the battalion sent its I Company to clear them out. At the front, the 1/358 continued towards Picauville, but came under German fire for the first time around 500 metres from the village. Colonel James V. Thompson, commander of the 357th IR, ordered the men to dig shelters, but he remained concerned about the situation to the regiment's rear: I Company had not successfully cleared out the chateau on the Isle-Marie. In addition, the engineers who were accompanying the infantry, who had to destroy the bridge over the Douve in Beuzeville-la-Bastille, had failed in their mission because they continued to come under fire from the opposite bank of the river. As the danger still existed, Colonel Thompson ordered the men to be on the defensive. In the middle of the afternoon, 1/358 came under a counter-attack, but it held firm and at 17:00, the four companies marched on Pont l'Abbé after an artillery bombardment conducted by the 344th Field Artillery Battalion. However, this attack only marked time and at 19:30, 1/358 and 3/358 began to dig shelters. The losses were heavy: 1st Battalion (1/358) alone suffered 17 killed, 93 wounded and 19 missing, a total of 129 men, or close to the size of a company! At this rate, the battalion would be eliminated in a few days.

77th Infantry Division

On 10 June, elements from a new German infantry division began arriving in the centre of the peninsula to reinforce the 91. (LL) Division, which had lost its leader. The 77. Infanterie-Division had been created a few months earlier, in January 1944, and was based in Brittany, at Saint-Malo. At the time, it was one of the weakest German divisions in the West, having only 8,508 men on 1 March 1944. However, it was somewhat reinforced, eventually totalling 9,095 officers and men, as well as 1,410 'Hiwis' (Eastern Volunteers), at the beginning of June. It only had two infantry regiments (although each had three battalions); Infanterie-Regiment 1049 (commanded by Colonel Bacherer) and Infanterie-Regiment 1050. Each of the regiments had forty machine guns. As for 8.1 cm mortars, IR 1049 had eight, while IR 1050 had seven. Each regiment had a 14th company that was equipped with three anti-tank guns and a 13th infantry company. IR 1049 had six Russian guns, but there were only two for IR 1050. The artillery regiment, AR 177, was very weak. Altogether, I./177 and II./177 had two batteries of four 10.5 cm howitzers each, meaning a total of sixteen howitzers for the two groups. The third group had three batteries each with four 8.8 cm Pak 43/41 guns and was the only motorised group.

The anti-tank group, Panzerjäger-Abteilung 177, included a company with twelve 5 cm anti-tank guns, and a company with twelve static 5 cm anti-tank guns, which would obviously remain in Brittany. On 7 June it was told to head for Normandy and the Cotentin Peninsula, and so prepared to leave Brittany (where it would be relieved by 5th Fallschirmjäger Division). The journey to the front line would take several days, with only the motorised elements of the division reaching Granville by 8 June. Two days later, on 10 June, some of the elements reached the Valognes sector, where they would reinforce the right flank of *Kampfgruppe* Keil (with two infantry battalions), but the rest of the division was still yet to arrive in full, and as will be seen later, it would do so in quite a dramatic fashion. (For more information, see *Normandy 1944* by Niklas Zetterling, pp. 229-31.)

The division was commanded by Generalmajor Rudolf Stegmann, who was born in East Prussia in 1894. He joined the Imperial Army in 1912 and was a Leutnant in the 141. Infanterie-Regiment at the beginning of the First World War, fighting on the Eastern as well as the Western Front. After the war he remained in the army of the Weimar Republic, and had reached the rank of major by the time Hitler came to power in 1933. He helped with the development of motorised infantry and commanded a motorised infantry battalion during the Polish Campaign. By the time of the French Campaign, and at the beginning of Operation Barbarossa, he was in command of the Infanterie-Regiment (mot.) 14, before successively taking command of the 2. Panzergrenadier-Brigade and the 36. Infanterie-Division (mot.).

4th Division heads north

On 10 June, two US regiments, the 8th Infantry Regiment (4th ID) and the 505th PIR (82nd Airborne Division) resumed their attack towards the north. The 8th Infantry Regiment were to advance towards the high ground at Eroudeville and so its three battalions set off in the early hours of the morning. The 2/8 advanced on Ecausseville, which had been abandoned by the Germans, having withdrawn to establish a line of defence at Montebourg. It then advanced towards the north-west, clearing a path to the south of Eroudeville, crossing the Montebourg-Le Ham main road in the early afternoon. It continued until it came up opposite the Germans, who were entrenched along the railway tracks, but as night fell, the battalion retreated back to the east of the main road.

Meanwhile, on the right, the 1/8, supported by tanks that were partly loaded with infantrymen, began its advance at 07:30, after an artillery bombardment. Moving along a path east of Ecausseville, the tanks came under anti-tank fire about 450 metres south of Eroudeville. The infantry dismounted and three German anti-tank guns were annihilated, the guns having belonged to elements of Sturmbataillon AOK 7.

This battalion had been formed in May 1943 as part of the 7th Army. Under the command of Major Messerschmidt, on 5 April 1944 he had a total of 1,106 men, divided into three infantry companies, each with twelve machine-guns, three Panzerschrecks (German bazookas) and two 8 cm mortars, with a heavy company possessing eight machine guns and two 7.5 cm infantry howitzers. The command company had four light Flak guns, two 5.5 cm Pak guns (anti-tank), and one of 7.5 cm Pak gun, four 12 cm mortars and fifteen machine guns. The battalion also had an engineer section. The term 'AOK7' meant that it depended on the command of the 7th Army. On 5 June 1944, it was positioned to the east of Cherbourg and had joined the right flank of Lieutenant Colonel Keil's regiment. The three anti-tank guns that 1/8 claimed to have destroyed were probably the three that belonged to the command company.

The German battalion was pushed back towards the main road by 2/8, but 250 metres away from it, 2/8 was halted by German elements in Eroudeville and to the north of the area. The Germans of the Sturmbataillon counter-attacked at 15:00 and 2/8 was pushed back several hundred metres. However, after five tank charges on Eroudeville, the situation was restored and the village was finally taken, with C Company protecting 2/8's eastern flank during the night.

To the west, on the left flank, 3/8 were delayed by heavy artillery fire and were late to attack as they attempted to outflank the houses to the east of the La Lande hamlet, which were held by the Germans who had halted the battalion here the previous night. However, the men came under artillery fire from the station during their advance, which took place at the same time as 1/8 and 2/8 were pushing back the infantrymen from the Sturmbataillon, and the 1/505 PIR were reaching the railway on the left. This allowed 3/8 to cross a small tributary of the Merderet at around 10:00, pushing the Germans back to the main road. In the evening, another attack allowed them to cross the road and reach midway between the road and the railway. However, caught under German fire from positions along the railway line, 3/8 was forced to retreat east of the main road.

By that evening, 8th Infantry Regiment had established their positions, which they would continue to hold without any further advance, until 19 June.

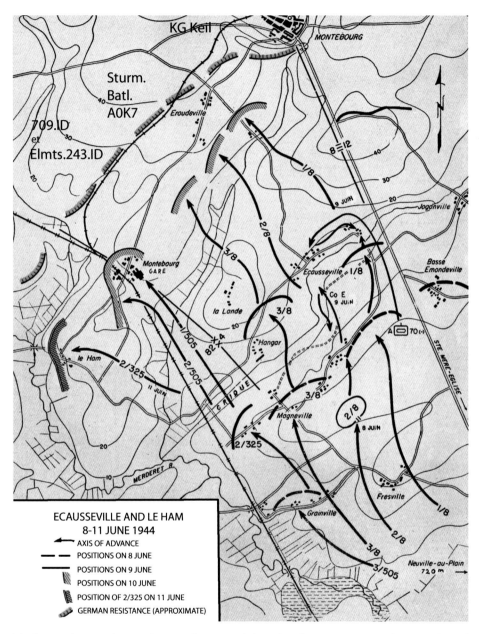

To the southwest of Montebourg, elements of the 4th Infantry Division (8th IR) and 82nd Airborne Division (2/325 and 3/505) fought for four days to gain ground in the sector of le Ham. The fighting was fierce. (US Army Map)

Kampfgruppe Keil: Montebourg

As we have seen, on 10 June, in the Montebourg sector, the American thrust was becoming more intense. An American reconnaissance tank arrived in the area, but upon reaching a barricade, the tank's crew (made up of a lieutenant and three men) was captured by a tailor and a cobbler from III./919 command company, who were only armed with a gun!

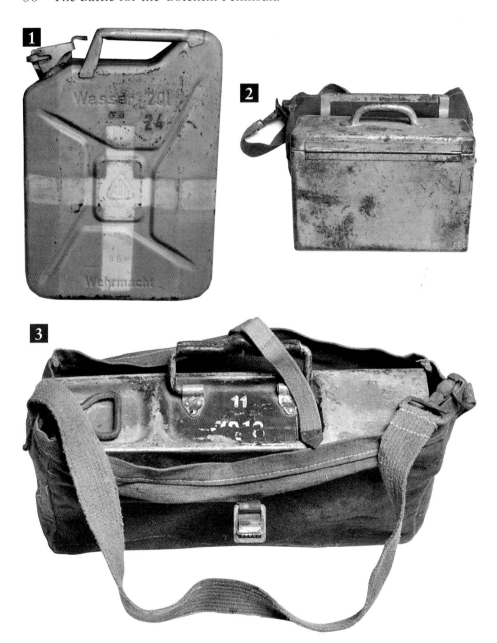

1. German jerrycan, or *Kanister*. Note the stamped inscription 'Wasser', and the white cross on the background *Afrika* colour, to indicate its use. It was found in 1987 in Montebourg, in the area where *Kampfgruppe* Keil fought. (Private collection/E.G./Heimdal)

2. German metal bag for a 350 N2 DKW motorbike, found in Bricquebec. This bag, like the *Kanister*, is painted in a sand colour, which was the custom in the German Army at the time. (Private collection/E.G./Heimdal)

3. German metal box for a machine gun belt (MG) in its carrying case, with shoulder strap. (Private collection/E.G./Heimdal)

Sunday, 11 June

90th Division attacks again

On 11 June the two regiments of the 90th Infantry Division resumed their attack. The 3/357 progressed 700 metres and cleared Amfreville in the morning. During the rest of the day, 1/357 attempted a wide flanking movement to la Lande in order to expel the Germans, but by nightfall had only advanced half the distance towards its objective.

Further south, the 358th IR provided the main thrust with Pont-l'Abbé as its goal. The town occupied a strategic position, being at the crossroads of four roads, with the one leading south making it possible to cross the belt of marshland and to push southwards. The Germans clung on to this sector as the three battalions, supported by artillery (four groups in total), attempted to overcome them. The mobile artillery barrage advanced 90 metres every five minutes. The three infantry battalions initially followed behind, but machine-gun fire coming from the eastern and northern outskirts of the village delayed the infantry who were advancing behind the artillery barrage. Pont-l'Abbé was partially surrounded by the beginning of the evening, but the advance was halted against the well-aimed German machine-gun fire and artillery.

On that day too, the 508th PIR was in line ready for a mission south of the Douve. It was organised into assault teams, supported by artillery from the 319th Glider Field Artillery Battalion, and by various other elements. It was ordered to cross the Douve by night at Beuzeville-la-Bastille, in the area between the Douve and the swampy Gorges meadows. They began at midnight during the night of 11-12 June, and the mission was a success, reaching Baupte by 08:00 the next morning.

A small trailer belonging to American paratroopers, found in 1988 at the farmhouse of La Moignerie in Amfreville, in the area of the 82nd Airborne Division. The tyres are original. (Private Collection/E.G./Heimdal)

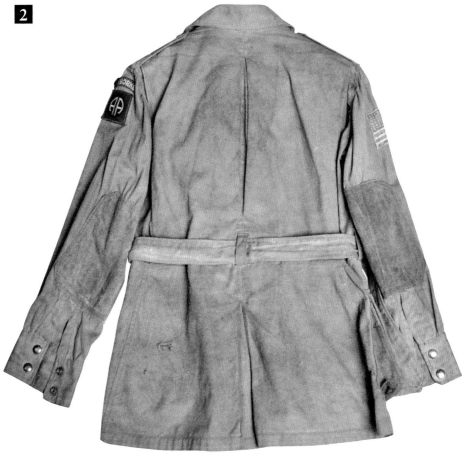

1. Detail of the trailer's tarpaulin showing its markings. (Private collection/E.G./Heimdal)

2. Parachute jacket of the 82nd Airborne Division, worn by a paratrooper from the unit who fought in this area. It was abandoned by its owner in July 1944, but remained in good condition. (Private collection/E.G./Heimdal)

3. Oberst Gerhard Triepel commanded the coastal artillery regiment HKAR 1261, which was positioned on the eastern coast of the Cotentin Peninsula. His headquarters were at La Pernelle. Following his determined exploits, he was promoted to the rank of Generalmajor.

At Montebourg

On 11 June, the US advance was even stronger in this sector. Montebourg was now under fire from the allied naval artillery, which would, unfortunately, devastate the area, as can be seen from photographs taken after the fighting. The town was destroyed and transformed into fields of ruins, making any daytime movements almost impossible for Germans defending it.

North of Utah Beach

While Montebourg constituted a veritable breakwater in the face of the 4th Infantry Division's assaults, the situation was no more favourable for the Americans along the coast, in the area where Colonel Hervey A. Tribolet's 22nd Infantry Regiment was engaged. On 7 June he had run aground against the batteries of Azeville and Crisbecq, with heavy losses. The Azeville Battery was defended by the 2./Artillerie-Regiment 1261, under the command of Hauptmann Dr. Hugo Treiber (who was positioned at the observation post in the Crisbecq Battery, from where he directed the fire) and Oberleutnant Hans Kattnig. This battery was part of the Heeres-Küsten-Artillerie-Regiment 1261 (HKAR 1261), an artillery regiment of eight batteries arranged on the east coast of the Cotentin Peninsula and placed under the command of Oberst (Colonel) Gerhard Triepel. The battery at Azeville had four French 105 mm Schneider guns placed under concrete casemates, two of which were particularly more imposing models (type H650), and the battery was located on the eastern edge of the village.

In front of the battery stood a heavy navy battery, the schwere Marine-Küsten-Batterie Marcouf, in the commune of Crisbecq, but near Saint-Marcouf. Consequently, this Crisbecq Battery was called Marcouf Battery by the Germans. It was a navy battery, hence its name Marine-Küsten-Battery (MKB), and not Heeres-Küsten-Battery (HKB), if it had been an army battery. Although dependent on the navy, it was integrated into Colonel Triepel's artillery regiment (whose HQ was in La Pernelle) and was numbered 3./1261. It was commanded by Oberleutnant zur See [a naval rank] Walter Ohmsen. It was a powerful battery, equipped with three Czech (Skoda) 210 mm guns.

Only two powerful casemates had been built, thus sheltering two of the guns while the third remained in the open. The guns fired against the Allied fleet at dawn on 6 June, sinking the destroyer USS *Corry* which had opened fire on Utah Beach. Had it not been hit by fire from the battery, the boat would have hit a mine anyway (see H. v. Keusgen, *Les Canons de Saint-Marcouf*, p.90).

4th Division re-launched the attack on the two batteries on 8 June, resulting in another failure and retreat after coming under Nebelwerfer and shell fire from Crisbecq. In the process, 1/22 lost more than half of its strength. The attack on the Azeville Battery was re-launched on 9 June at 11:00 by 3/22, having been preceded by 1,500 rounds of artillery fired by the 44th Artillery Battalion. After a difficult advance, Captain Joseph T. Samuels (I Company) sent Private Ralph G. Riley out with a flamethrower; artillerymen were burned alive and, at 14:30, Oberleutnant Kattnig surrendered - not before the guns at Crisbecq had fired a final salvo on Azeville to try to dislodge Captain Samuels and his men. On 10 June, an attack by the 22d IR, along with 3/22, concentrated mainly on the fortified support position of the chateau at Fontenay. The 3/22 had only engaged two companies, including L Company, which had already lost 159 men. Pinned down by the machine guns firing from the now-ruined chateau at Fontenay, the battalion fell back under the German fire, abandoning seventy men who either perished under the bombardment or were captured. Throughout the area, aerial bombardments attempted to crush German positions, some of which were heavily fortified. The Crisbecq Battery was at death's door, but managed to hold out for six days before being destroyed.

The Azeville Battery

1

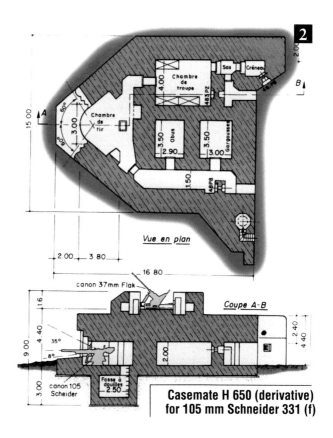

1. A view of the two powerful H 650 casemates. Traces of camouflage are still visible in the embrasure. (E.G./Heimdal)

2. Plan of a large H 650 casemate. Housing a 105 mm gun, it was surmounted by a concrete tank equipped with a 3.7 cm Flak gun. (B. Paich/Heimdal)

3. One of the casemates taken after the fighting. Note that the Flak gun is still visible. (N/A)

Vue en plan

canon 37mm Flak

Coupe A-B

canon 105 Scheider

Fosse à douilles 2.50

Casemate H 650 (derivative) for 105 mm Schneider 331 (f)

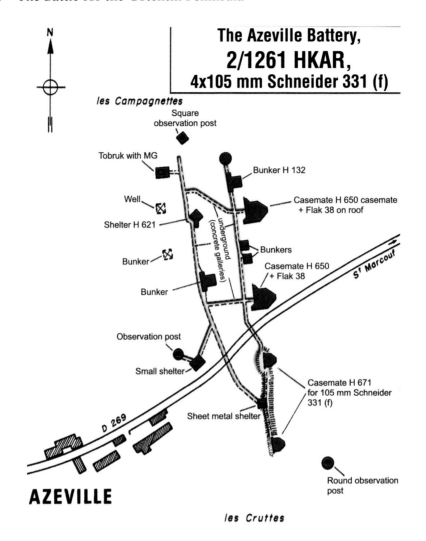

The Azeville Battery,
2/1261 HKAR,
4x105 mm Schneider 331 (f)

N

les Campagnettes

Square observation post

Tobruk with MG

Bunker H 132

Well

Casemate H 650 casemate + Flak 38 on roof

Shelter H 621

underground (concrete galleries)

Bunkers

Bunker

Casemate H 650 + Flak 38

S* Marcouf

Bunker

Observation post

Small shelter

Casemate H 671 for 105 mm Schneider 331 (f)

D 269

Sheet metal shelter

AZEVILLE

Round observation post

les Cruttes

Plan of the Azeville Battery. Today, the battery is open to the public. (B. Paich/Heimdal)

Evacuation of the Crisbecq Battery

At the Crisbecq Battery on the afternoon of Sunday, 11 June, Oberleutnant zur See Ohmsen was called to his post. From Cherbourg, his commander Konter-Admiral Hennecke, Seekommandant, asked the naval gunner to try and break through with the rest of the battery's artillery and the remaining soldiers from 6./919 who had retreated there, and make their way to the German lines, which were trapped in front of the Americans only 8 kilometres to the north.

The departure had to be discreet, meaning Ohmsen could not destroy the guns. Shortly after midnight, in the battery's main garrison, of the 311 men from MKB Marcouf, and the 95 men from 6./919, Ohmsen collected only 78. As Helmut von Keusgen notes (*Les Canons de Saint-Marcouf*, Heimdal, 2005):

Men were crushed by fatigue, tension and the psychological pressure that comes from continuous fighting. The soldiers, mostly elderly, were at their limit. Almost all of the troops and officers were wounded. Only seven of Ohmsen's twenty-four non-commissioned officers survived, and almost all were injured. However, they still carried four seriously wounded men on stretchers, but would leave another twenty-one behind, Ohmsen also leaving one of his two medics and a non-commissioned officer, who had volunteered. The six days of fighting for the MKB Marcouf would cost the lives of 307 German soldiers.

A total of 126 American prisoners would remain locked in the building so as not to betray the Germans' departure.

Cautiously, step by step, Ohmsen's little group stumbled in the field dotted with corpses on this clear, late spring night. In the distance, on all sides, fired the crackle of incessant battle. The soldiers passed through the hamlet of Pierreville before they reached the flooded area. Slowly, they advanced until the cold water reached their hips. In some places, where they found ditches, the water reached up to their chests. The stretchers carrying the moaning wounded had to be carried on the shoulders of the strongest men. This incredible journey through the uneven flooded terrain to the German lines near Aumeville lasted 8 kilometres and involved more than three hours of walking, a true Way of the Cross. Here is the last sentence of Ohmsen's report from 1 July 1944: 'The discipline and combative morale of the garrison was good to the end, with few exceptions.'

The men from the battery managed to reach the German lines near Aumeville. The exhausted soldiers received medical care and food, and were able to rest there for two days.

Crisbecq Battery

One of the H 683 casemates after the fighting, showing one of the three 210 mm. The American soldier allows the viewer to see the enormous size of the casemate. (US Army)

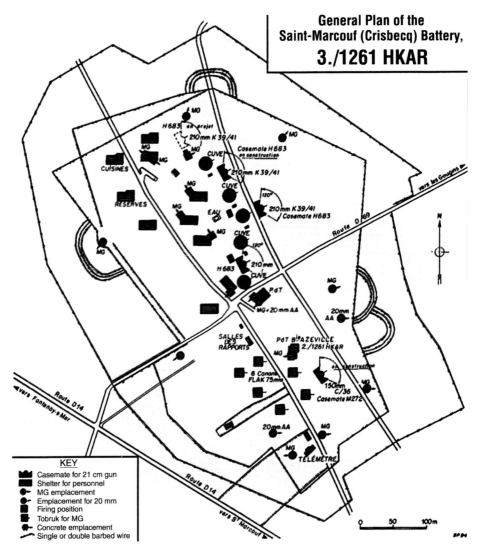

General Plan of the
Saint-Marcouf (Crisbecq) Battery,

3./1261 HKAR

A plan of the battery, which was called MKB Marcouf by the Germans. Two type H 683 casemates were built, a third was under construction, and a fourth was being planned. (B.aPaich/Heimdal)

Monday, 12 June

Crisbecq and Ohmsen

Taking advantage of the arrival of the 39th Infantry Regiment on 11 June, the following day General Collins ordered one of the 9th Infantry Division's three infantry regiments (the bulk of which would be committed to the west Merderet), to take the coastal battery of Marine de Crisbecq. One of the regiment's battalions, 2/39, commanded by Colonel Harry A. Flint prepared for a hard fight against this seemingly impregnable fortress, only to find it abandoned, except for the 21 seriously wounded Germans and the 126 American prisoners. However, the

The casemates were destroyed after the fighting. Here, the roof slab has fallen into the firing chamber. As in Azeville, the site is open to visitors and the exploration of these two sites is strongly recommended. (J. Bavay)

regiment's other two battalions, 1/39 and 3/39, had to fight hard in order to take the last German positions between Ravenoville and Fontenay. The following day, 13 June, a communiqué from the OKW (Commander-in-Chief of the Wehrmacht) emphasized Ohmsen's particularly fierce resistance: '... The Heeres-Küsten-Artillerie-Abteilungen 1254, 1255 and 1201, the Marine-Küsten-Artillerie-Batterien Marcouf, La Pernelle and Longues particularly distinguished themselves.'

On 14 June, Oberleutnant zur See Ohmsen joined the coastal battery at Morsalines, around 2.7 kilometres away. He was celebrated as a hero, and on that day was decorated with the Naval Artillery Badge (Marine-Artillerie-Abzeichen, created on 24 June 1941 to reward the action of navy gunners), as well as the Ritterkreuz, the prestigious Knight's Cross of the Iron Cross, as a reward for his exploits and those of his fellow combatants. A Berlin newspaper published the following article to galvanize the population, who still hoped that the Allies will be kept in check in Normandy:

At the proposal of Commander-in-Chief of the Navy, Grand Admiral Dönitz, the Führer awarded the Knight's Cross of the Iron Cross to Oberleutnant Walter Ohmsen for his courageous and decisive exploits in the fight against the invading fleet. Ohmsen was the first to report the Invasion and thus was responsible for spreading the warning along the coast of Western Europe. On his own, he immediately engaged his battery to the last extremity in order to fight the invading fleet, despite the fire of enemy battleships and violent bombardments. He then sank a cruiser and a ship loaded with ammunition, damaging many vehicles. Through his heroic personal commitment, along with his courageous men, and despite heavy losses, he continued to resist using his particularly important battery, even though he was surrounded by the enemy. He thus provided the possibility of bringing reinforcements and prevented the widening of the bridgehead and the breakthrough planned by the enemy along the north coast of the Cotentin Peninsula. In the first phase of the battle against the Invasion, Ohmsen was wounded as he fought at the front of his men against the landing units, and defended himself against parachutists who had landed behind his battery. He abandoned his battery only on the orders of the Kommandeur of his sector and after its total destruction.

Note that it is claimed here that Ohmsen was the first to report Operation Overlord and not Major Pluskat, as was depicted in *The Longest Day*. At 02:20 on 6 June, Oberleutnant z.S. Ohmsen had alerted Konter-Admiral Hennecke regarding the parachutists landing nearby. Before 05:00, when dawn was breaking on the horizon, he saw the allied fleet and launched his 210 mm shells as early as 5:52 - three minutes before the first allied shots. At that hour, Major Pluskat was not at his post at Sainte-Honorine-des-Pertes, but with a lady friend in Caen...

Another article was published about Ohmsen's exploits on 17 June, but he was captured by the Americans at Cherbourg on 26 June 1944 and remained a prisoner

The first picture taken after being awarded the Knight's Cross of the Iron Cross on 14 June 1944. Oberleutnant zur See Walter Ohmsen is surrounded by two other artillerymen from his former garrison. Their wounds were healed and they were washed, shaved and wearing new uniforms. Despite being surrounded, the report would soon reach Germany, where the photos would be published a few days later for propaganda. Another image with a close-up of Ohmsen appeared in the navy's newspaper, *Gegen Engeland*, at the end of June. (BA)

until 15 March 1946. After the war, Walter Ohmsen entered the Bundesmarine on 16 March 1956 with the rank of Kapitänleutnant. He retired on 30 September 1967 with the rank of Fregattenkapitän and died in Kiel on 19 February 1988, aged seventy-seven.

In the West – Objective Pont-l'Abbé

To the west of the Merderet, the 90th Infantry Division was still showing a lack of any effectiveness, its advance remaining weak on 12 and 13 June. Each day of combat, the 357th Infantry Regiment, which lacked any experience, lost 150 men - the strength of a company! Faced with the determined resistance of the Germans, the Americans bombarded Pont-l'Abbé on 12 June at around 17:00. In the night of 12-13 June, the Americans finally entered the empty and ruined town, but which remained an important crossroads.

Following the failure of his offensive, Major General Jay W. McKelvie was relieved of his command and replaced by Major General Eugene W. Landrum. This new general was fifty-three years old and was born in Penascola, Florida, on 6 February 1891. He joined the army in 1910, becoming a second lieutenant in 1916, and serving with the American Expeditionary Force in Russia in 1919. He attended various military schools between the two world wars and was stationed in Alaska at the beginning of the Second World War, in the Alaskan Defense Command. He was promoted to brigadier general in March 1942 and then major general in March 1943, taking command of the 87th Infantry Division in October that year. During Operation Overlord he was placed on the US VII Corps's staff in case he was needed to replace another general who might fail in his command. This was the case on 12 June when he took direct command of the 90th Infantry Division. He was an experienced general, but would initially have little impact in the course of the battle. With a round face and a prominent

Major General Eugene W. Landrum took command of the 90th Infantry Division on 12 June 1944, following the dismissal of Major General Jay W. McKelvie. He worked hard to reorganise the division after its previous failures. He retained command until 28 July when he, in turn, was relieved of command, becoming commander of the replacement infantry training centre in Texas in October 1944. He died on 24 July 1967. (US Army)

nose, along with a short, athletic silhouette, Landrum was not a charismatic leader. Wearing a coat that was too big for him and often carrying a cane, his appearance was more pessimistic than optimistic in nature. His voice lacked expression, but his words encouraged the hope that things would be better. He had to try and galvanize a division that was lacking in any experience and would tour his units in the coming days in order to give them the confidence to allow them to go back in to the lines more efficiently, which would be the case in the weeks to come (see G. Bernage, *Objective La Haye-du-Puits*, Heimdal, 2012). For now, the 90th Infantry Division would be reduced to a secondary role, involving the protection of VII Corps' flank.

In light of this failure, Major General Collins was forced to put an already experienced, elite division, into the lines: the 82nd Airborne Division. For the time being, it was this division who would resume the main thrust of the offensive in the sector.

The 9th Division Finally Arrives

VII Corps had expected the arrival of a new division, the 9th Infantry Division, on D-Day + 4 (10 June), to be assembled as soon as possible in order to be engaged in the sector around Colomby and Orglandes. Following the bad results of the 90th Division, and after the dismissal and replacement of its leader, General Collins decided to modify the initial plan. For his attack to the west, he now had to engage two divisions. The 82nd Airborne Division was put back in the lines for this attack. It would have to concentrate on the banks of the Douve to the north, west of the Merderet, in order then to advance west. Finally, the 9th Division would cross the Merderet and advance head-on with the paratroopers from the 82nd. As we will see, the 9th Division was already an experienced unit.

The 9th Infantry Division would play an important role in the Battle of the Cotentin Peninsula. Set up in July 1918 in Sheridan, Alabama, it was still in the USA when the Armistice was signed on 11 November 1918 and was demobilised that December. It was reactivated on 1 August 1940 and trained at Fort Bragg in

North Carolina, where it participated in major manoeuvres in September 1941. It continued its training, among other amphibious activities, in Chesapeake Bay, east of Washington, in August 1942, before gradually leaving the USA between September and November 1942 to serve in North Africa. From March 1943 it took part in the fighting in Tunisia and entered Bizerte on 7 May 1943. In August 1943 it saw action in Sicily, fighting around Troina, Floresta and Randazzo, on the road to Messina. Both of these campaigns provided valuable experience for the men. The division returned to Britain from

Fabric badge of the 9th Infantry Division.

November 1943 for further training and attached to VII Corps, it landed at Utah Beach on 10 June 1944.

The division was commanded by Major General Manton S. Eddy. Born in Chicago, Illinois, on 16 May 1892, the son of George Manton Eddy and Martha Bishop Sprague, he joined the army in 1913. A second lieutenant in 1916, he fought in France as a first lieutenant in the 4th Infantry Division's 39th Infantry Regiment. Wounded in battle, he ended the war as the commander of a machine gun battalion. In 1919 he commanded the 1st Battalion of General Pershing's escort regiment. He took courses at the US Army Infantry School at Fort Benning and then at the US Army Command and General Staff School (1932-1934). He then served as a professor of military science and tactics at Riverside Military Academy, Georgia. In March 1942, he was a brigadier general and second-in-command of the 9th Infantry Division stationed at Fort Bragg. Three months later he commanded it in North Africa and Sicily. He would keep command in Normandy until August 1944, when he took command of XII Corps, staying there until the end of the war. From 1950 to 1955, he commanded the 7th Army in Europe until his retirement. He died on 10 April 1962 at Fort Benning.

The division comprised of three infantry regiments. The 39th Infantry Regiment was commanded by Colonel Harry A. Flint and included three battalions: 1/39 was commanded by Major Henry P. Tucker, 2/39 by Major Franck L. Gunn and 3/39 by Lieutenant-Colonel Robert H. Stumpf. The 47th Infantry Regiment was commanded by Colonel George W. Smythe, with 1/47 commanded by Lieutenant Colonel Dearn T. Vanderhoef, 2/47 by Lieutenant Colonel James D. Johnson and 3/47 by Lieutenant Colonel Donald C. Clayman. The 60th Infantry Regiment was commanded by Colonel Frederick J. de Rohan, with 1/60 (codename Red) commanded by Lieutenant Colonel William C. Cox, 2/60 (codenamed White) by Lieutenant Colonel Michael B. Kauffman, and 3/60 (codenamed Blue) by Lieutenant Colonel Arden C. Brill. The division had four artillery groups: the 26th, 60th, 84th and 34th Field Artillery Battalions. These were armed with 105 mm howitzers, except for the 34th, which had 155 mm howitzers. The division also had tank, anti-tank and artillery reinforcement

Major General Manton S. Eddy took command of the 9th Infantry Division in the summer of 1942 in North Africa, where he led it into combat, as he also did in Sicily. His experience and that of his men would be invaluable for the offensive to the west and the cutting off of the Cotentin Peninsula. (US Army)

units attached to it. General Eddy's deputy head of the division was Brigadier General Donald Armpriester Stroh, whom we will find at the head of the 8th Infantry Division from 13 July 1944, in the Haye-du-Puits sector (see G. Bernage, *Objective, La Haye-du-Puits*, Heimdal).

However, on 12 June, the 82nd Airborne Division's units were being reorganized following losses sustained since the night of 5-6 June. The 507th and 508 PIR, as well as the bulk of the 325 GIR had been relieved on 10

Major General Eddy is seen here in the area around Cherbourg giving his orders for the ongoing battle. (N/A)

June after crossing the Merderet. The effective force of the two paratrooper regiments, according to Major Ruppenthal, amounted to only 50-60 per cent of their initial force. The 505 PIR and 2/325 GIR would remain in line in the Ham sector, opposite the *Kamppgruppe* Keil, until the morning of 13 June, when they would be relieved by the 359th Infantry Regiment. As we have seen, the 508th PIR intervened south of the Douve on 11 June and had reached Baupte; an important position for future operations south of the marsh belt, which would take place at the beginning of July (see G. Bernage, *Objective La Haye-du-Puits*, Heimdal).

In the evening of 12 June, General Eddy received a message from VII Corps warning him to be ready to make his way to the bridgehead west of the Merderet as soon as possible. However, he was missing a regiment, the 39th Infantry Regiment, which was temporarily attached to the 4th Infantry Division in order to help with the attack on Quineville.

As of 12 June, the 91. Luftlande Division, which was positioned in the centre of the peninsula, on the right flank of the *Kampfgruppe* Keil, had already lost 2,212 men either killed, wounded or missing (according to the report by AOK 7 - Ia Nr.3116 / 44g.Kdos on 15 June 1944). The losses of this division, committed in the centre of the Cotentin Peninsula, would continue to increase to 85 per cent of its infantry, 21 per cent of its artillery potential, 76 per cent of the men in its engineer battalion and 48 per cent of the men in its Panzerjäger anti-tank group, from 6-24 June (according to the report by AOK7 - Ia Nr.3454 / 44 g.Kods on 27 June 1944).

Montebourg – none shall pass!

Meanwhile, to the north, on the RN13 road, Montebourg remained a solid barrier, blocking any progress by the 4th Infantry Division. On the German side, Hauptmann Simoneit, Kampfkommandant of Montebourg, lost one of his officers, Leutnant Hilscher, and was wounded himself by a shell burst. Hauptmann Wenk, leader of the tank battalion, then became Kampfkommandant. The front had been held for four days at Montebourg, in spite of the increased voracity of the American attacks. The extreme importance of this position was emphasised by the daily report from the 7th German Army, which announced: 'Cherbourg wird bei Montebourg verteidigt' (Cherbourg will be defended at Montebourg). The position was the cornerstone of the front, and Doctor Max Simoneit was at the heart of its resistance.

Simoneit had fought in the First World War and was seriously wounded. Afterwards, he practised as a psychologist and founded the Wehrmachtspsychologie (military psychology). He was appointed secretary of state at the OKW, but asked to join the front. An experienced soldier, he joined Infantry Regiment 919, commanded by Lieutenant Colonel Keil in January 1944. Despite his age (fifty) and the after-effects of his wounds (which hindered his walking), Hauptmann-Doktor Simoneit took command of the Stabs-Kompanie (the regiment's command company). He mixed with his men and put his work into practice by attaching great importance to their psychological training, showing that the moral behaviour of each individual was crucial for the group as a whole. As we have seen, during the first days of fighting he took command of the Montebourg sector. After being wounded on 12 June, General von Schlieben proposed his elevation to the rank of major and that he should receive the Knight's Cross of the Iron Cross, which he was awarded on 26 June for his outstanding courage. On his way back to Germany (he was evacuated before the peninsula was cut off), while on board a hospital train, Simoneit was wounded twice again by air strikes. He ended the war in a military hospital and, after 1945, was a professor in Schleswig-Holstein.

On 12 June, east of Montebourg, the 12th US Infantry Regiment continued its advance between Montebourg and Saint-Floxel, gradually pushing back the *Kampfgruppe* Rohrbach (commanded by Colonel Rohrbach, the head of Infanterie-Regiment 729). The American advance pushed the *Kampfgruppe* back 1 kilometre beyond the initial front line. In the morning, General Marcks (commander of the 84th German Army Corps) arrived at *Kampfgruppe* Keil's CP (located north-east of Montebourg and west of that of KG Rohrbach, see maps). He ordered the retreat along a line passing by the southern edge of Fontenay-sur-Mer and Dangueville, during the night of 12-13 June. The III./922 and III./739 fell back in the darkness, unbeknown to the Americans.

Tuesday, 13 June

On 13 June, Colonel Rohrbach arrived at Keil's CP. He announced that the Americans had broken through near Saint-Floxel and he expected the front line to withdraw to the high ground north of Montebourg. However, he was ordered to take back the former positions. Following a week of fighting after the IR 919 had received the first hit, Keil was able to draw up an initial assessment:

- The standard of the troops had improved and had become used to fighting.
- The Americans, notwithstanding their superiority in terms of resources, had not succeeded in making any meaningful progress towards the north.
- The Allies had total air superiority.

By the end of the day, and at the end of a week of fighting, on D-Day + 7 the American bridgehead in the Cotentin Peninsula remained very narrow, faced with a determined German resistance. It was an elite division, the 82nd Airborne Division, who would move the front; from Pont-l'Abbé to its objective of Saint-Sauveur-le-Vicomte. According to the plan, they now had to push forwards towards the sea.

The Pont-l'Abbé sector

Due to the failure of the 90th Division, this was now a day of rest. General Collins gave orders for the resumption of the offensive the following day. The 90th Infantry Division would remain in line first and stick to the northern flank. The 82nd Airborne Division would attack along the axis of the Pont-l'Abbé/Saint-Sauveur-le-Vicomte road, advancing with two of its regiments on either side of this main road: the 507 PIR on the right (north of the road) and the 325 GIR to the south. The 9th Infantry Division would move forwards to the centre of the line, between the 82nd and the 90th.

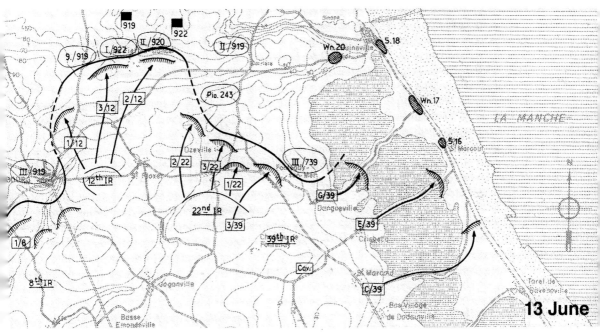

Thanks to maps published by Major Rupenthal giving the American positions day by day, and those of Lieutenant Colonel Keil that give the German positions, we are able to corroborate the two and provide a synthetic map showing the positions of each of the protagonists. Thus, from 12 June General Barton launched his 4th US Infantry Division on the attack between Montebourg and the coast. On the left, the 8th Infantry Regiment remained in a defensive position in front of Sturm-Battalion AOK 7. To the east, the 39th Infantry Regiment began a difficult advance towards the coast, in the midst of the flooded ground, in order to climb up to Quinéville. In this sector, the Azeville Battery fell on 9 June. As for the Saint-Marcouf (Crisbecq) Battery, this was evacuated during the night of 11-12 June by Oberleutnant zur See Ohmsen and his men, after a heroic resistance. In the centre, the 12th Infantry Regiment and the 22nd Infantry Regiment would play the most decisive role in pushing back the German front on either side of Saint-Floxel. To the west of Montebourg and to the east of Saint-Floxel, the German front was 'up in the air'. (Heimdal)

3

Saint-Sauveur-le-Vicomte: 14-15 June

Wednesday, 14 June

North of the Douve

The attack was re-launched on 14 June, north of the Douve River, with two and then three divisions, thus giving a considerable advantage to the American offensive. From south to north, they were the 82nd Airborne, 9th Division and 90th Division.

507th PIR

In the Pont-l'Abbé sector, one of the 90th Division's regiments, the 358th IR, had to take the crossroads located to the west of the town, on the main road. At 08:50, two of the regiment's battalions advanced on either side of the road, attacking a small German support point located before the crossroads that controlled the road coming from Valognes and Orglandes, the D24. The crossroads were taken and held at the beginning of the afternoon, but because it was close to the Douve Valley, it still came under German (88?) fire from the southern shore. The regiment was relieved at noon by elements of the 507 PIR, who had begun to advance as planned, on the right. The two lead battalions advanced on both sides of the road to the south of Bonneville, where they would take up positions in the evening.

North of the 358 IR, the 359 IR began to veer to the right (northerly), opening a breach between the two regiments through which the first line regiment of the 9th Division (60th Infantry Regiment) arrived. It proceeded to advance north of Gottot, first with a single battalion, the 3/60. This new division was soon able to extend its front line, while the 82nd advanced in a line to the south on a narrow front along the main road, and the three regiments of the 90th Division headed to the north, thus allowing the 9th Division to come up in the centre of the manoeuvre.

The 9th Division then marched on Hameau Renouf, with the sector located to the north-west of Orglandes as its objective. However, the 3/60 came under fire from small arms and mortars, as well as artillery. Despite this, Hameau Renouf was reached and taken at 18:00. With the reinforcement of the 2/60, the two battalions reached the Orglandes road, the D24, at nightfall. Faced with the fear of German reinforcements arriving from the south – thanks to reports of the 265. Infanterie-Division coming from Brittany - General Eddy ordered the 60th IR to resume the advance the next morning at 05:00 and move as fast as possible.

To the north, one of the regiments of the unfortunate 90th Division, the 359th IR, encountered further problems. Heading towards Orglandes, the two

1. A soldier from the 82nd Airborne Division, most likely the 325th Glider Infantry Regiment, heading for Amfreville. (D. François)

2. Crossroads, south of Amfreville, where a monument commemorates the parachutists of 6 June. The author is seen examining the signposts, indicating the objectives of 14 and 15 June (Gourbesville), as well as La Bonneville. (Erik Groult/Heimdal)

leading battalions, 2/60 and 3/60, lost contact and German infantrymen succeed in infiltrating through, meaning the 3/60 was practically surrounded for parts of the day. The northernmost regiment, the 357th IR, also faced problems. Its most northerly objective was Goubesville (north-west of Amfreville), but the regiment suffered several blunders in the support it received: a missed aerial bombardment at 14:00, before another was to be prepared for 18:00, but unfortunately, many of the shells fall on the men themselves. There was a further barrage at 19:30 before the 3/60 entered Gourbesville at 22:30. However, the regiment was unable to clear it out and the village remained in German hands.

Keil holds Montebourg

A new day of fighting began on 14 June. At 07:00 a motorcycle liaison officer arrived at Keil's CP and handed the lieutenant colonel an order to attack, even though Keil remained sceptical. The attack was scheduled for 07:00 and he was only now receiving the order. The liaison officer was unable to say where Rohrbach's CP was currently located, and the artillery remained silent. Suddenly, at around 10:00, elements of two battalions from *Kampfgruppe* Rohrbach retreated to Keil's CP. They had not received the attack order and were being pushed back by the Americans. Only III./919, at Montebourg, had attacked, but it had done so without any artillery support and was consequently driven back, although it did inflict some casualties on the Americans. III./919 retreated to Montebourg and 9/919 fell back to Hill 69, near Keil's CP. This meant that

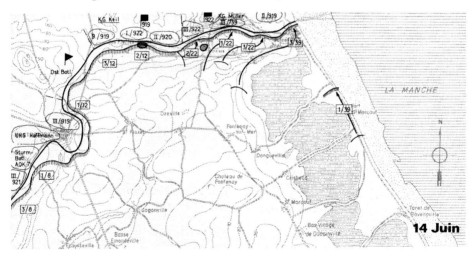

At midnight on 14 June, Montebourg was more than ever the cornerstone of the German front before Cherbourg, forming a salient. East of Montebourg, opposite the 12th Infantry Regiment, Lieutenant Colonel Keil reconstructed a front line with the remains of two battalions (including a battalion of Georgian volunteers) and the remains of a company. Further east, Lieutenant Colonel Müller's *Kampfgruppe* was based in the Sinope Valley, which was relatively hemmed in along part of the river's course. This *Kampfgruppe*, made from the remains of three battalions, was facing the 22nd Infantry Regiment and the 3rd Battalion of the 39th Infantry Regiment (a regiment of the 9th US Infantry Division that was temporarily detached from the 4th US Infantry Division). Quinéville came under the assault of this last battalion after hard fighting which included the use of flamethrowers. (Heimdal)

there was now an American salient that pushed out between Saint-Floxel and Montebourg, the latter now more than ever a cornerstone of the front, enclosed to both the south and east by the Americans. With no news of Rohrbach, Keil took over the two battalions and reconstructed a front line. General von Schlieben was informed of the situation and disbanded the *Kampfgruppe* Rohrbach. Keil was then commanded to take the entire southern front under his command. General Hellmich (who commanded the 243. Infanterie-Division) arrived at Keil's CP. According To Keil:

Upon arriving at my CP, General Hellmich asked me if I was able to hold the southern front. I said yes. He asked me if I could take charge of Rohrbach's sector. There were no forces available to carry out a counter-attack and to re-establish our former situation. We had to keep our current positions.

The front line extended along the approximate route of the Montebourg-Quinéville road, running along a line of high ground. To fulfil his mission, Keil had the following units at his disposal:

-   To the west of Montebourg, and linking up with the 77. Infanterie-Division, the Hoffmann *Unterkampfgruppe* was made up of the Sturm-Battalion AOK7 and the remains of the IR 1058.
-   For the defence of Montebourg: under the command of Hauptmann Wenk, with his Pz.Ers.-Abt. 101 (two companies of French tanks), two companies of paratroopers, III./919 (without the 9/919).
-   On the high ground north of Montebourg: Division-Kampfschule (the division's combat school) was in position near Hoffmann's CP, which received Rohrbach's former staff and had a powerful radio.
-   Under the direct control of Keil, between Montebourg and the railway, an Ost-Battalion was entrusted to him on 14 June (this was a Georgian battalion, the 795th, which lost a company), 9./919, I./922 and II./920 (battalions from the former *Kampfgruppe* Rohrbach). The sector boundary lay to the east of Keil's CP. The next section, under the command of Lieutenant Colonel Müller, extended as far as Quinéville and the coast. Keil also had artillery, particularly the s.Artillerie-Regiment mot. Seidel (which shared its CP with Hoffmann). Seidel positioned his 1st group north of Montebourg, and his 2nd group (minus one battery), further to the east, near Keil's CP. Moreover, Keil also had Major Rasmer's Nebelwerfer-Regiment 100 at his disposal. This was a regiment of rocket launchers; a weapon particularly feared by the Allies. In addition, some of the coastal artillery batteries were able to intervene in the sector.

To combat the tanks, Keil also had Pak guns from the Panzerjäger-Abteilung 709, as well as flak guns from the Flak-Regiment Hermann.

In the afternoon of the 14th, Keil's CP was bombed and two Pak guns were destroyed. As a result, Keil pulled back his CP to the west of Saint-Martin-d'Audouville. Rasmer, who commanded the Nebelwerfer-Regiment 100, set up his own CP close by. Meanwhile, Quineville and Aumeville were also heavily bombed.

Thursday, 15 June

The attack on the Douve

The attack pushed west, with the 82nd Airborne Division advancing the quickest, for reasons we will see later. The 325 GIR was in front and it was there that the German resistance would be the weakest. Due to its rapid advance along a narrow front, which thus gave it greater control, in the afternoon General Collins ordered the 325 GIR to advance to the hills at Rauville-la-Place, 900 metres east of Saint-Sauveur-le-Vicomte. On its right (north), the 507 PIR was relieved by the 505 PIR, which would slow down the advance. However, it would try to hold the same line, but with its right flank curved right in order to maintain contact with 90th Division's 60th. The 505 PIR arrived on the line south of Reigneville at nightfall, the front thus forming a circular arc from the Douve Valley in the south, before curving northwards to the most westerly point at Rauville.

In the centre was the 9th Infantry Division. General Eddy's division first re-launched its attack with the 60th Infantry Regiment at 05:00 on 15 June, but soon came up against an obstinate German resistance. Shortly after the start of the attack, the Allies were confronted with a counter-attack as sixteen panzers were spotted moving south from Orglandes. The 60th IR reacted by placing bazookas and 57 mm anti-tank guns on the front line, which put 'three Mark III tanks' out of action, according to Major Ruppenthal (*Utah Beach to Cherbourg*). For its part, the 60th IR lost two of its anti-tank guns. This was obviously a counter-attack by Panzerjäger-Abteilung 243, which of the four German divisions present in the Contentin Peninsula, was the only anti-tank unit equipped with German armoured vehicles. As we have previously seen from studying General Hellmich's 243. Infanterie-Division (on which it depended heavily), this anti-tank group did indeed have fourteen Marder 38s and ten Sturmgeschütz IIIs, according to the division's delivery report from May 1943 (BA-MA Rtt 10/349). There was no 'Panzer III' in the Cotentin Peninsula, which by this time was an obsolete tank. On the other hand, the ten assault cannons were built on a Panzer III chassis, which Major Ruppenthal may have included when he said 'sixteen', a 'recount' may include some of the Marders. In any case, only three Sturmgeschütz IIIs were destroyed and identified. This heavy counter-attack also shows the Germans' desire to prevent the peninsula from being cut off, as the 77. Infanterie-Division had just arrived in the sector.

At 09:00, the 60th IR arrived 450 meters from the Orglande-La Bonneville road (D330), where ... *four tanks and an infantry battalion counter-attacked strongly on the right of 1st Battalion (1/60) which retreated 500 meters from the road. The battalion suffered losses, including the commanders of companies A and B, which disappeared, but the 2nd Battalion (2/60), which was just behind, opposed the enemy threat and regained half of the lost ground.* (Ruppenthal, *Utah Beach to Cherbourg*, p.130).

From that morning General Eddy altered the axis of 60th IR's attack by ordering it to head westward towards Reigneville, while on its right, the 359th IR would head north-west. A gap then opened up between

505th PIR

the 60th IR (9th Division) and the 359th IR (90th Division), which allowed the 47th Infantry Regiment (a second regiment from 9th Division), to come into the line. Its objective was the plateau west of Orglandes, which had previously been the objective of the 60th IR. Thus, shortly after noon, the 47th IR came up into the line, its 1/47 at the head, which deployed its companies in a way as to allow 2nd Battalion to come up on the right of 1/47 from 16:30. However, the situation was more worrying on the northern flank, where enemy fire from Orglandes threatened the rear on the right, momentarily halting 1/47. It resumed its advance in the late afternoon, helping 3/47 on the right. The latter was then exposed and stretched out to the right, also in a circular arc. But the advance was quick and the regiment had managed to reach its objective by nightfall.

Further to the right (north), was General Landrum's 90th Infantry Division. Next to the 9th Division, the 359 IR attacked to get past Orglandes and cut off the Orglandes-Urville road, but it only managed to advance 900 metres and remained far from its objective. On its right, the 3/357 fought all day to capture Gourbesville. The 3/358 attacked to the right of 3/357, with orders to take the crossroads located to the south of Urville, at the same time of the 359 IR's attack. However, on this exposed northern flank, 90th Division's successes remained very limited.

As Major Ruppentahl notes: 'As a consequence, the units on the American right flank met with the strongest enemy opposition every time, while the units on the left flank advanced with relative ease.' The American front thus formed a circular arc curving northwards from Rauville to Gourbesville, where it connected with the solid German front line at Montebourg. The advance would now take place at Saint-Sauveur-le-Vicomte, the following day's objective, and the 'door' that would lead to the breakthrough to the sea.

Montebourg is still held

At dawn on 15 June, the 9/919 retreated before returning to action. Its leader, Oberleutnant Kaehler, was killed while trying to retake his former CP with his

German equipment found on the Cotentin Peninsula after the fighting. It includes a Mauser K98 rifle with its sight, an MG34 rifle maintenance box, a maintenance box for an 8.1 cm mortar (right), and an armoured vehicle headlight complete with black out and antenna base. (Private collection/Heimdal)

men. The breach along the Montebourg/Saint-Martin-d'Audouville road was now closed and it was at this time that the German artillery crushed an American attack along the Ost-Battalion and II./920's lines. Lieutenant Colonel Müller established his CP at Hill 45, 800 metres north of Lestre. The evening would remain calm.

However, the Americans had suffered heavy losses due to the German artillery and the Nebelwerfer. They set out to recover their dead and their wounded, using heavy machine gun fire to provide cover as they went about their task. This caused a panic among the Georgians from the Ost-Battalion, who began to retreat. Keil explained to them that they were not under attack, and sent the Georgians back to the front line.

Friday, 16 June

Montebourg: Wendorf counter-attacks

On 16 June, in the Montebourg area, the 4th Infantry Division attacked Keil's former CP, which was located in the quarry near Hill 69. Hauptmann Flokerzi, who commanded II./920, was killed in action. Keil received III./729, one of the battalions from 709. Infanterie-Division's three infantry regiments, as reinforcements. This compensated for the losses of the valiant 919. Infanterie-Regiment and he would launch it in a counter-attack in the afternoon. The attack was supported by Seidel's guns and the Rasmer's rocket launchers, but the battalion's commander was wounded at the start of the attack and it went no further. Keil would now launch the experienced Oberleutnant Wendorf in the battle, who before arriving in Normandy, had received the wound badge 1st class (*Verwundeten-Abzeichen*) in Gold. After receiving command of 6./919, he had been placed at the head of the Divisions-Kampfschule. Along with the men from his new unit, Wendorf formed an assault group, taking the lead himself, in order to re-take the quarry. He achieved his objective, but was wounded in the process and had to retreat with his men.

Hesitations and decisions in the German Command

On 16 June, the German Command emerged from a long period of hesitation, which facilitated the Americans' success in their offensive towards the west. As we have seen, when the US VII Corps had attacked the Merderet on 9 June, progress was slow. But this first success could lead to a breakdown of the German forces, as had already been envisaged. Among LXXXIV. Korps, the 7. Armee (Dollmann) and even the Heeresgruppe B (Rommel), the belief would be that they would abandon the peninsula and withdraw towards the marshes. This would be favourable defensively speaking, as all the divisions would then be firmly in position to block any breakthrough to the south. But Hitler wanted to defend Cherbourg, although it was questionable whether or not this 'fortress' had enough men to do so. The current positions of his front lines seemed insufficient.

There was hesitation between the 'hold at any price' command coming from the OKW and Hitler, and the southwards reorganisation advocated by the intermediate levels of command. These hesitations considerably complicated the chain of command. Although Keil's mission in the Montebourg sector was clear and he was able to lead an effective defence, the hesitations concerning the west of the peninsula meant that actions were often uncoordinated. Telephone lines were broken, radio links were generally scrambled and orders were transmitted by liaison officers. Units began to retreat southward, only to be recalled to the north again, going back and forth in the middle of the American offensive, which only resulted in skirmishes rather than any solidly coordinated attacks. This toing and froing affected the confidence of the ordinary soldier, who consequently began to lose hope and was thus more inclined to surrender.

By 16 June, the situation was becoming clearer, but it was too late. On that day, for the first time, a noise like a motorcycle was heard going across cross the sky: V-1 rockets were on their way to hit England, and these 'secret weapons' would help to strengthen somewhat the confidence of the German soldier. That day also saw a change in the decisions made by the High Command. At 10:00 Rommel arrived at his Command Post for a conference and made his decision: 'I give permission to separate the groups. The wish to hold everything means to lose everything.' Consequently, a number of the four divisions would head north for Cherbourg, while the rest would withdraw south to hold the line in the marshes. However, an order from the OKW ordered him to hold the current front line at all costs. He said, 'Facing an order from the Führer, I am powerless!'

However, the redistribution of forces was under way. The 709. Infaterie-Division and Grenadier-Regiment 922 from the 243.Infanterie-Division would join the Quinéville-Valognes-Le Ham sector (with KG Keil) and reassemble in a *Kampfgruppe* Cherbourg under the command of General von Schlieben. To avoid any uncertainty, the Ob West (German High Command in the West) stated that responsibility for the northern part of the Cotentin Peninsula and the port of Cherbourg was entrusted to the commander of the 709. Infanterie-Division, Von Schlieben.

The bulk of the 77. Infanterie-Division (without its GR 922), the 91. Luftlande-Infanterie-Division and the 243. Infanterie-Division were placed under the command of the latter's Kommandeur as *Kampfgruppe* Hellmich. Their objective was to break through towards the south. The arrival of a *Kampfgruppe* from the 319. Infanterie-Division, which occupied the Channel Islands, failed due to Hitler's change of orders. However, by 16 June the Americans had already penetrated deep behind the right flank of Generalleutnant Stegmann's 77. Infanterie-Division. The division was to the south of Valognes, but would have to pull back to the Portbail-Doville line. Stegmann hesitated; maybe it was already too late. He tried to contact the commander in Cherbourg, but the liaison officer there told him that the situation in the port did not inspire him with confidence. He believed the arrival of new troops would not lead to an improvement in conditions but rather to complications, because there were already a great number of troops in the city and there were not enough supplies for any more units.

Stegmann decided to continue the plan of withdrawing to the south. He received his mission for 17 June and would face his destiny:

Pull back towards Saint-Sauveur, Bricquebec and Barneville. Use infantry and armoured vehicles to stop any attempt to hinder withdrawal. Order of march: GR 1049, GK1050, Artillery-Abteilung 177, 177. Panzerjäger-Kompanie (anti-tank), Pionier-Batallion 177 (Engineer), 177th Signal Battalion.

Saint-Sauveur-le-Vicomte

General Collins outlined the objectives for the day: they must attack the whole front, from the Douve to Gourbesville. The 82nd Airborne Division would march on Saint-Sauveur-le-Vicomte, while the 358th Infantry Regiment (90th Division) would attack north-west of Gourbesville, and the 9th Division would advance between the two divisions in order to seize the Reigneville/Hauteville-Bocage/Orglandes/Gourbesville line. This last division would advance with a total of four infantry regiments in line (from north to south): 39th IR, 359th IR, 47th IR and 60th IR. The 359th was a regiment from 90th Division which was attached to the 9th Division for this attack and, as we have seen, the 90th would advance on the right with only one regiment, the 358th, the 357th being in held in reserve.

The outcome of the battle would be decided in the area around Saint-Sauveur-le-Vicomte. The attack by the 82nd and 9th Divisions started between 05:00 and 08:00, but in the 82nd Airborne Division's sector, supported by A Company of the 746th Tank Battalion, the 325th GIR broke the German lines and the men from the glider regiment would drag the division's other two other regiments along in their wake. By noon, the 325th GIR, the 505th PIR and the 508th PIR held the eastern bank of the Douve and were facing Saint-Sauveur and its powerful feudal castle. From this slightly steep eastern bank, the Americans saw the Germans withdrawing and General Ridgway asked permission to cross the river to take advantage of this situation and establish a bridgehead in Saint-Sauveur. He had

Aerial view of the ruined Saint-Sauveur-le-Vicomte. One can see the imposing mass of the medieval castle that dominates the Douve Valley, whose course can be seen in the foreground. The engineers' temporary bridge was erected to the left of the new bridge, which is seen here on the site of the present bridge. This aerial photograph was taken by the US Army a few weeks after the fighting. It is taken in the direction of the American offensive, looking west, towards the sea. (NA)

already been carrying out attacks on the roads leading to the village, to the north, west and south, and he now asked the 325th GIR to stand ready to cross the river.

The authorisation arrived at 13:00 and the river crossing was completed without any great opposition. By nightfall, a broad and solid bridgehead had been established around Saint-Sauveur-le-Vicomte, with a defensive perimeter of 1,200 to 2,000 metres. In the evening, tanks arrived in the small ruined city and the bridgehead would form an essential base for the offensive.

The 9th Infantry Division launched its attack in the early morning and due

508th PIR

to the good news from Saint-Sauveur regarding the German withdrawal, the order quickly came to push on more vigorously. At 11:30 General Collins called General Eddy to his divisional headquarters and told him to advance his 47th IR and 60th IR on Sainte-Colombe, while the 39th IR will provide the protection for his flank. Eddy ordered the 60th IR to advance to the Douve with its three battalions.

The 3/60 had left at 05:00 and had been confronted with heavy fire. The 1/60th had broken through the German's defensive line and come across a field hospital, which also contained wounded Americans, before clearing out Reigneville-Bocage. Under Lieutenant Colonel Michaels B. Kauffman, the 2nd Battalion of the 60th Infantry Regiment (2/60), rushed over the terrain from 11:00, to the crossroads of the D2 main road from Valognes to Saint-Sauveur-le-Vicomte. E Company was at the front, followed by F Company, accompanied by heavy machine guns, but the German machine-guns positioned in houses below the crossroads opened fire on the lead company. A platoon from E Company crossed the road and headed for the houses, managing to kill several Germans and taking sixteen or seventeen prisoners. The troops then had to arc northwards in order to avoid some panzers - probably those of Panzerjäger-Abteilung 243, the only ones available in the area - and entered Sainte-Colombe unopposed.

This village allowed them to reach the Douve which at this point, upstream of Saint-Sauveur, is not an important river. It divides here into three branches, each crossed by a bridge, leading to Néhou on the western shore. It was decided to cross the river as fast as possible, despite the likely presence of mines, with E Company in the lead, along with tanks from B Company, 746th Tank Battalion, which carried some of the infantrymen. The 2/60 made straight for the river, but the third bridge had been blown up and so the tanks were forced to turn around. However, as the infantrymen advanced along the roadway, they were hit by German shells and light rifle fire from Néhou. Despite the retreating tanks, E Company succeeded in crossing to the west bank, which it held even though it came under German fire. Sadly, their ammunition was running out. F and G companies also tried to cross but came under fire and when some of the men were hit, the others had to bury them. The situation at this small bridgehead was precarious. Lieutenant Colonel Kauffman asked General

The medieval castle at Saint-Sauveur-le-Vicomte, now restored, looking from the bridge over the river Douve, where the 325 GIR crossed. (G. Bernage)

Collins for reinforcements for his battalion, but the latter replied that although the 3/60 would come to support him, he must hold on at all costs for the time being. In addition, Kauffman brought back a 2.5 ton truck loaded with ammunition, thus remedying the ammunition shortage. The 3/60 would join the exhausted 2/60 during the night, thus allowing the advance to resume again the following morning.

Colonel George W. Smythe's 47th Infantry Regiment had received its orders from General Eddy at 13:30: its objectives were Golleville and Sainte-Colombe. The regiment first passed Biniville and reached the main road (the D2), where it took up positions. This success here was due to the one already achieved at Saint-Sauveur-le-Vicomte. Finally, the 39th Infantry Regiment cleared the land west of Gourbesville, while the 359th IR (90th Division) advanced to the top of the Orglandes road and stopped there. On this northern flank, the 397th IR tried to bypass the 359th IR on the left, to pass Orglandes on this side, but a German counter-attack prevented them. Any further movement in this area was now blocked by the time night fell.

From Pont-l'Abbé to Saint-Sauveur-le-Vicomte, 14 - 16 June

1. From 14 June, flanked on its right wing by the 9th Infantry Division, the 82nd Airborne Division advanced westward from the village of Pont-l'Abbé, where the 90th Infantry Division had suffered heavy casualties. Seen here are men from 82nd Airborne Division in the middle of the ruined village.

2. Map showing the progress of three American divisions towards their next obstacle, the Douve River, from 14 to 16 June. On 15 June, the 505th PIR, in front of a weakening German resistance, relieved the 507th PIR and took up position south of Reigneville, while the 325th Glider Infantry was approaching Saint-Sauveur-le-Vicomte. At noon on 16 June, three regiments from the 82nd Airborne Division (the 505th Parachute Infantry, the 508th Parachute Infantry and the 325th Glider Infantry) were trapped on the eastern shore of the Douve, facing the town of Saint-Sauveur-le-Vicomte. As the German retreated, VII Corps HQ allowed Major General Ridgway to exploit the situation and he immediately ordered a bridgehead to be formed on the other side of the river, which would be achieved by the 505th PIR and 508th PIR, supported by elements (A Company) from the 746th Tank Battalion.

1

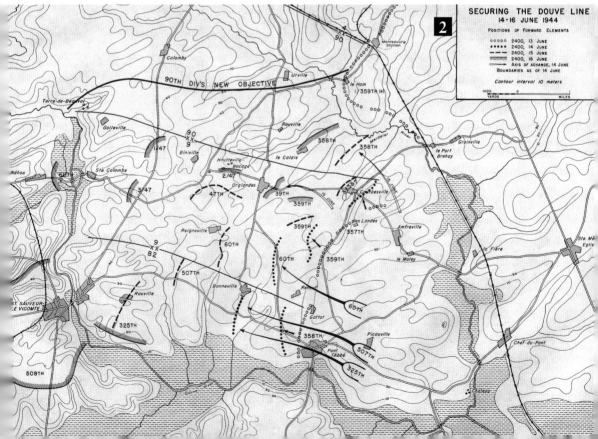

2

SECURING THE DOUVE LINE
14-16 JUNE 1944
POSITIONS OF FORWARD ELEMENTS
ooooo 2400, 13 JUNE
••••• 2400, 14 JUNE
───── 2400, 15 JUNE
━━━━━ 2400, 16 JUNE
━━► AXIS OF ADVANCE, 14 JUNE
BOUNDARIES AS OF 14 JUNE

Contour interval 10 meters

1000   0
YARDS   MILES

1. Lieutenant Kelso C. Horne (1st Platoon, I Company, 508th PIR) poses with his Garand rifle. Despite ten days of fighting, the US paratroopers showed exceptional spirit.

2. During its advance towards Saint-Sauveur, a section of paratroopers takes shelter in a ditch, ready to open fire. In the background, a German truck covered in camouflage paint straddles the road.

3 & 4. Two relatively old German soldiers have surrendered and are being escorted by a paratrooper, as civilians look on. (NA/Heimdal and US Army - Map: Historical Services of the US Army)

Saint-Sauveur-le-Vicomte, 16 June

1. This aerial photograph, looking east, shows a ruined Saint-Sauveur-le-Vicomte, dominated by its medieval castle with its mighty keep (top left). In the background can be seen the road coming from Pont-L'Abbe, and the course of the Douve river (which is visible above the castle). In the top right, can be seen the crossroads that will feature in the following images.

2 & 3. Paratroopers from the 505th PIR advance down rue Bottin-Desylles, towards the station, which was still in German hands.

4 & 5. These photographs follow on from images 2 and 3. This platoon leader, with FM BAR on his shoulder, is sitting on the wing of a car listening to the report from one of his men in another position.

1, 2, 3, & 4. Still on rue Bottin-Desylles but on the opposite pavement, and from behind, the anti-tank gun (seen in image 2) and the car can still be seen in the background. The house of number 50 (now number 56) was still dilapidated in 1984, but has since been renovated. Its seventeenth-century door frames have been reconstructed, although the small panes of glass have disappeared and the door itself has lost its knocker. (NA/Heimdal)

Saint-Sauveur-le-Vicomte, 16-20 June

This famous photograph shows Lieutenant Colonel Vandervoort leaning on his crutch, in the middle of the ruins at Saint-Sauveur-le-Vicomte. In the background, can be seen the road sign indicating the direction of Haye-du-Puits, to the right. It would take another month to reach it. This photograph was taken looking east. (DF/Heimdal)

The same place, rue du Vieux Château, today. (EG/Heimdal)

Lieutenant Colonel Ben Vandervoort in his M-43 field jacket.

This picture was taken in the same location on 16 June, but looking westwards; on the left is the house visible on the right of image 1. Lieutenant Colonel Vandervoort continues to advance, supported by his crutch, but his jeep stayed behind. (DF/Heimdal)

The same place with a slightly different vantage point. GIs are seen clearing the rubble. (DF/Heimdal)

The same location (images 4 and 5) today. On the right hand side can be seen part of the castle's fortified wall, now uncovered by the houses which had hidden it until 1944. (EG/Heimdal)

Near Saint-Sauveur-le-Vicomte on 16 June. The Americans have recovered a German Borgward vehicle and have transformed it into an ambulance. (DF/Heimdal)

Four days later, on 20 June, US engineers had set up a bridge over the River Ouve at Saint-Sauveur-le-Vicomte, allowing vehicles to advance to Bricquebec and the north-west of the Cotentin Peninsula. (DF/Heimdal)

The site of the temporary bridge, south of the current one, to the south-east of the castle. (GB)

Saint-Sauveur-le-Vicomte, after the fighting

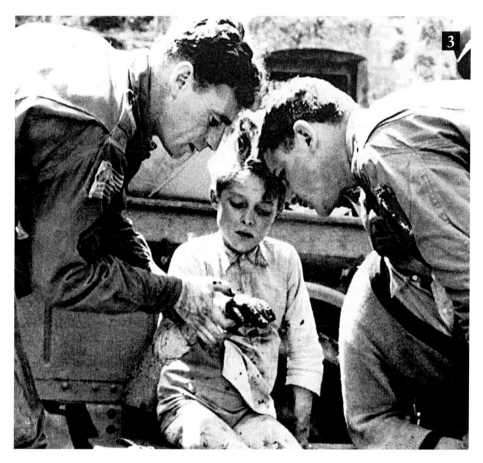

1. After the battle, men from the 82nd Airborne Division are seen resting under a school blackboard where they have written in chalk: 'The town (or remains) of St. Sauveur-le-Viscomte is hereby liberated as of now by US soldiers'.

2. Once again, the civilian population had paid a heavy price following the bombing and fighting. A pickup truck being used as an ambulance has brought a wounded boy to the medical station. The boy's name was Jean-Louis, who was ten years old, and had been wounded in the legs and his arm.

3&4. Young Jean-Louis being tended to by US medics.

1. Further ahead, medics and doctors care for the injured.

2. The horror: a paratrooper rescues a little girl from the ruins, who was sadly not as lucky Jean-Louis. (US Army)

4

The Cutting of the Peninsula: 17-18 June

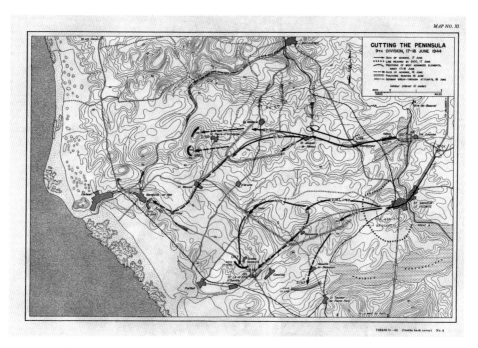

This map of the US Army's actions shows the final phase of the cutting off of the Cotentin Peninsula by the 9th Infantry Division on 17 and 18 June, from Sainte-Colombe (60th IR) and Saint-Sauveur-le-Vicomte (47th IR). To the north, the 60th Regiment passes through Saint-Jacques-de-Néhou and advances on Barneville. To the south, the 47th Regiment advances towards Portbail.

Saturday, 17 June

Montebourg sector

Despite the loss of these two general officers, intelligence reached Keil's CP in the Montebourg sector informing him that the Americans had penetrated westward into the 91. Luftlande-Infanterie-Division's sector. In the afternoon, Seidel's artillery regiment stumbled south, joining the retreat. Thus, with this American breakthrough, the right flank (to the west) of the *Unterkampfgruppe* Hoffmann had disappeared, and now the latter unit was threatened. In this crisis situation, Keil's CP received the order to withdraw to the planned line in front of Cherbourg. The withdrawal was to take place over three days. After a week of relentless resistance at Montebourg, *Kampfgruppe* Keil had the honour of being quoted in the OKW's (Oberkommando der Wehrmacht) daily communiqué: 'During the fighting on the Cotentin Peninsula, a *Kampfgruppe* commanded by Lieutenant Colonel Keil and Pioneer-Battalion 191, commanded by Captain Bonekamp, particularly stood out'.

The 9th Division heads west

On this day, the 9th Infantry Division made spectacular progress with two of its regiments, the 60th Infantry Regiment, to the north, from Saint-Jacques de Néhou, and the 47th Infantry Regiment, to the south, from Saint- Sauveur-le-Vicomte.

In the north, according to the history of the 60th Infantry Regiment: 'On the morning of 17 June, the men of the 60th continued their advance, eyes reddened, un-shaven, but with a very high morale. The regiment's situation was that of an isolated spear piercing through German positions'. As Major Ruppenthal states:

The 60th Infantry Regiment departed at 06:00 in columns of battalions from its bridgehead at Sainte-Colombe. The enemy had evacuated Néhou and the American columns followed the Nehou-Barneville highway (D42 then D242) without meeting any opposition other than that of small groups. The 1st Battalion (1/6), last in the column, captured a complete group of German field artillery.

The artillery in question was one of the 77. Infanterie-Division's artillery groups.

Thus, the 3rd Battalion (3/60) marched on Barneville, while 2/60 and 1/60 headed west to Saint-Pierre-d'Arthéglise, towards the line of hills overlooking the Barneville – Bricquebec road, including Hill 145 and Hill 133 (see map). The 1/60, which captured the German artillery group, was the last in the column. These three battalions from the 60th Infantry Regiment would be reinforced by 1st Battalion, 39th Infantry Regiment (1/39), which at the time was near Saint-Jacques-de-Néhou, where the Germans, who occupied the church, were removed by a shell. The steeple had collapsed and while one German soldier was killed, another was wounded and taken prisoner, along with five of his comrades.

1 & 2. In the commune of Sortosville, the Germans built a radio-guiding station for the Luftwaffe at Hill 145, which was the highest point of the sector. It was only makeshift at first, but was then concreted in the summer of 1941 and a Knickebein antenna was installed. When the Americans (2/60) arrived there on 18 June, there were only two Germans on the site and one of them was killed. The site was added to the Supplementary Inventory of Historic Monuments on 25 September 1990. It features a large bunker (seen here), the Knickebein KX 'factory' (the cubed constructions on the roof are ventilation chimneys). Above the door, a bas-relief shows the Luftwaffe eagle with the inscription: *Erbaut unter Adolf Hitler im Kampf gegen England 1940* (built under Adolf Hitler during the war against England, 1940). From this site is a magnificent view of the whole area and it was from this high ground that the American artillery fired down on the retreating German columns on 18 June. (J. Bavay)

According to the history of the 60th Regiment:

The 3/60 reached its first objective successfully: Néhou, which the enemy had just evacuated. While it was temporarily halted at its second objective, the Blandamour crossroads (on the D90 - crossing the Bricquebec/Saint-Sauveur-le-Vicomte north-south road, and the other east-west axis), 2nd Battalion outflanked it on the right (north), and continued the advance.

However, the advance was quickly slowed down as it passed through this dense grove by snipers, who had camouflaged themselves in the hedges that lined the road leading to Saint-Jacques-de-Néhou. The infantrymen consequently had to climb onto the Sherman tanks from 746th Tank Battalion and, under their combined fire, were able to advance to the crossroads.

By nightfall, the four battalions were in line between the Douve and the sea, but instead of stopping as darkness arrived, they were ordered to continue. Progress

A column of the 60th Infantry Regiment, 9th Infantry Division, crosses Saint-Jacques de Néhou heading west on 17 June. Here we see a fork in the road; the road on the left will be used by the 1/60 and the road on the right (the D42), by the 3/60, whose men can be seen here. The church bell tower was destroyed, the Germans were entrenched, and before dawn the next day (18 June) furious fighting would take place in the hamlet of Jacquin, to the north-east of this village. (Heimdal)

had been so great on that day that General Collins ordered the 9th Division to continue as far as possible throughout the night, in view of the imminent cutting off of the peninsula. At 22:10, General Eddy was in his jeep and overtook the command group of the 60th Regiment, shouting: 'We're going to go all night!' The 3/60 received the verbal order to continue as far as Barneville, in order to cut off the road from the coast.

Further south, the progress made by the 47th Infantry Regiment was equally satisfactory. The regiment's three battalions had also departed the Saint-Sauveur-le-Vicomte sector early in the morning, sporadically clashing with a few German troops in the process. They reached Besneville, their first objective, before then reaching Saint-Lô-d'Ourville and Portbail. At 22:00, 1/47 reached the small village of Huanville, north of the Olonde chateau; Saint-Lô-d'Ouville was very close, and the battalion crossed the Barneville/Haye-du-Puits road, definitively cutting off the road to any German units. It even reached the sea at Portbail harbour, even though the official breakthrough will not take place until the next day in Barneville. Meanwhile, K Company, 3/47, arrived at Saint-Sauveur-de-Pierrepont.

The deaths of General Stegmann and General Hellmich
According to German sources, at 06:00 on 17 June in the town of Les Perques, where the D-50 (the road leading from Bricquebec to Portbail) crosses the

D127 (leading south to Saint-Sauveur-de-Pierrepont, crossing the threshold of the Cotentin), known as the 'Vente aux Saulniers crossroads', General Rudolf Stegmann's staff car was parked at Hill 86, accompanied by his driver and his orderly. To the north of the crossroads is a fountain and a further road running north-west, which services the commune of Perques. A large beech tree, now removed, was situated at the south-west corner of this intersection and covered the area with its thick foliage. It was there under this canopy that the general had stopped, sheltering from the Allied planes lurking in the sky. Further ahead, the road was banked by a network of hedges surrounding the fields, and a small house stood near the fountain. The general had spread out his maps on the bonnet of the car, whose roof had been folded back. He took stock of the roads his 77. Infanterie-Division were using to retreat, after their withdrawal southwards had finally been authorised by Rommel. They must take care not be surrounded in the pocket that was now being formed in the Cotentin Peninsula.

Suddenly, a grenade flew by and exploded, killing the general and his driver, although the orderly was unscathed. The latter would afterwards describe the drama and its circumstances by declaring 'the death of this great leader was a great misfortune for Germany'. He also pointed out that General Stegmann had been killed by 'a very small fragment to his heart'. But what were the circumstances of this tragedy? In *Utah Beach to Cherbourg* (1948), Major Ruppenthal claims that the general was killed on 17 June by an American fighter-bomber at the Perques crossroads, and although the bomb missed the crossroads itself, the ensuing shrapnel is what killed him. American troops would later discover his body on the morning of 19 June as they moved north.

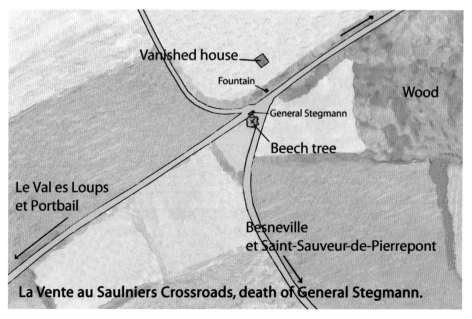

The Vente aux Saulniers crossroads, where General Stegmann was killed on 17 June 1944. (E. Groult/Heimdal)

The crossroads today, looking towards Bricquebec. On the right is the road leading to the 'Vente aux Saulniers', in the direction of Saint-Sauveur-de-Pierrepont. On the left, at the end of the road from where this picture was taken, were the fountain and house (now disappeared) where the two American paratroopers took shelter. The large beech tree at the corner of the crossroads on the right has also disappeared. The general's car was in the middle of these crossroads. (GB)

However, local witness statements, which may be more precise (although not always) provide another angle. These include André Hamel's *9th US Division US d'Utah Beach à Goury* (self-published, Briquebec, 1994), as well as Jeannine Bavay's research and *La Voix du Dungeon* (in particular n°41, June 2004). This last publication recalls the testimony of several senior citizens who lived through these events, including Edmond Brémond and Auguste Rioult, as well as Pierre Lhomme and Louis Moulin's father, all of whom lived close to the crossroads. Here is the testimony of the latter:

In the days following 6 June, American soldiers – by which I mean parachutists – were hiding in the Vrétot countryside (a nearby commune, north of Perques). One of them arrived at Louis Rioult's, a farmer at the top of Malassis (where General Hellmich's headquarters were located) who was especially known for his tractor as he was the milkman for Perques and Vrétot. Two others, or perhaps this one and another, were found in a small, destroyed house, located in a field belonging to Jules Hennequin, Mayor of the Perques, on the roadside at the Carrefour de la Vente aux Saulniers and the Portbail road. Jules Hennequin was mowing the grass and cutting the hay and the border with a scythe. He heard a whistle and turned, followed by a second whistle that came from the little house. Then a paratrooper came and made him understand that he wanted to eat. Jules Hennequin handed over his own snack to the American, but there were two hiding there, and so Jules Hennequin brought food in secret. There is still water in the fountain at the foot of the slope today.

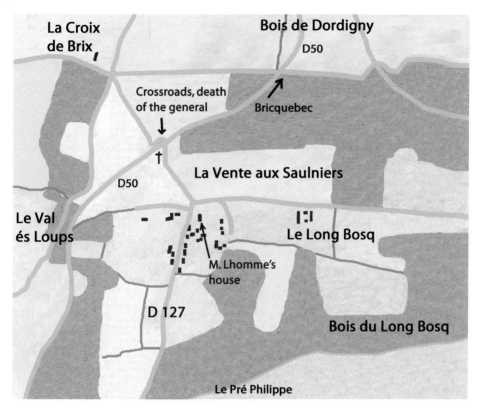

General map. The Brix Cross crossroads, to the north, was where the paratroops hid. You can also see the Long Bosq farm where the general's corpse was first brought, then Monsieur Lhomme's house where he was brought back to, and where the Americans discovered him. (E. Groult/Heimdal.)

This means that General Stegmann's car would have been parked just below the house where the two American paratroopers were hiding. Realising the situation, the Americans could have launched the grenade that killed the general and his driver. This theory is all the more convincing because it is difficult to see how a fighter-bomber could have seen the vehicle and the three men under the beech tree's foliage, which is among the most opaque. A 'small fragment' corresponds well to that of a grenade. On the other hand, why would they have been satisfied with firing a single grenade? Did they retreat after this attack, fearing reinforcements would arrive?

Among the stories surrounding the death of General Stegmann, it was widely reported that 'it was a paratrooper who had done the deed...' (see A. Hamel, p. 81). According to some, the two paratroopers may have been sent there on a 'secret mission', to kill 'the general'. It is true that there was another general nearby; General Hellmich was at his headquarters in Malassis, very close to this crossroads. Chance would have done the rest, one general in the place of another, especially since many thought that it was General Hellmich who had been killed there ... What is more, among the 'legends' reported by André Hamel, one brave lady told him: 'The American's name has never been known, and he had no luck ...

He was so tired that he had leant on his loaded gun. The gun went off and blew off his head...' However, Hamel states that a similar accident occurred in a house in Perques, but when the American troops arrived, this time the soldier had drunk too much cider and Calvados. This is a well-known story and was told to us by Madame Blanche Delacour, now 83-years -old, who was living at her parents' house in Malassis. Although the two stories vary slightly, neither include the solider killing the general.

It was a nurse from Bricquebec who received the orderly's testimony regarding the death of the general, a testimony communicated to Pierre Lhomme, who saw the general's body after it was brought to his home by horse drawn carriage, although it was first taken to the Long Bosq farm. A witness reported to Charles-Henri Grillard (the mayor of Bricquebec at that time) that the general was tall with red hair. Monsieur Tardif, a refugee at the Long Bosq farm (the body had been originally placed by the Germans in the little house), said he saw the general's body in the farm's courtyard, his magnificent boots protruding from the sheet covering the body. Two days later, on 19 June, the body would be in an American 4x4 vehicle near Pierre Lhomme's home. General Rudolf Stegmann is now buried in the German cemetery of Orglandes, a few kilometres south of the place where he died. His body thus remains in the Cotentin Peninsula, where his death at the la Vente aux Saulniers has become almost a myth for the people of the Bricquebec region.

1. The Long Bosq farm where General Stegmann was first brought in a cart. (Jeannine Bavay)

2. Monsieur Lhomme's house. The general was brought back here, before the Americans found his body and loaded it onto a 4x4. (Jeannine Bavay)

3. Grave of Generalleutnant Rudolf Stegmann, Kommandeur, 77.ID, in the Orglandes German military cemetery. (E.G./Heimdal)

This was a black day for the German troops in the Cotentin. A little farther on, in Canville-la-Roque, General Hellmich was also killed in an air attack while leading his division. He was killed on the same day in an area between Portbail and Saint-Sauveur-de-Pierrepont, connected to the north by the D70, to the crossroads where General Stegmann was killed. This means that of the four German generals who had commanded divisions in the peninsula, three were killed within a fairly close range: General Falley on 6 June at his CP near Picauville; General Stegmann on 17 June at Les Perques; and General Hellmich at Canville on the same day. The troops were made leader-less at a crucial time. The only one who remained was General von Schlieben, who would hold the fate of all the surrounded troops in his hand. Like Stegmann, General Hellmich was buried at the Orglandes military cemetery, a few kilometres from the location where they perished.

The grave of Generalleutnant Heinz Hellmich, Kommandeur, 213. ID, also killed on 17 June and buried at Orglandes. (E.G./Heimdal)

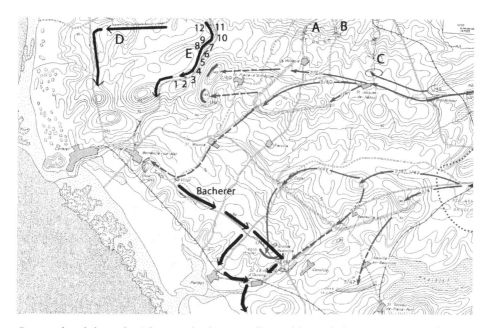

German breakthroughs: These took place on all possible roads between 03:00 and 04:30 on 18 June. They were stopped by Americans roadblocks established on crossings over the Scye, a stream that ran east/west, which the troops had to cross at several points. This was the case at Pont-Saint-Paul (A), on the D50 from Bricquebec, between Les Perques and Valdecie, where a roadblock was established with minefields and demolition charges on the bridge. Identical defensive positions were taken south of the Pont du Moulin de Gonneville (B). The II. and III./GR 1049 attempted the route via these two points, north of where General Stegmann had been killed the day before. The 1st Battalion, 39th IR (1/39) occupied a position in the hamlet of Jacquin (C) at 04.30 when a German column from GR 1049 arrived from the north. Surprised, the battalion retreated to the east of Saint-Jacques-de-Néhou on the D42. However, the retreating columns used all of the possible routes, including the road (D) from Vrétot and heading towards Sénoville, then Barneville and the south. The terrain was rugged, almost 'mountainous', with summits of 145 metres, even though the sea is close by. The hilliest axis was the Bricquebec/Carteret road (E), the D902. The Germans suffered considerable losses, which were published by Jean Barros, according to the 9th Infantry Division's operations report from 14 June to 1 July 1944. Thus: **1.** 1 truck, 1 howitzer, 6 horses, 1 caisson. **2.** 1 truck of 2.5 tons, 3 bicycles. **3.** 1 tracked vehicle. **4.** 1 mortar, 4 horses, 1 ammunition van. **5.** 2 semi-tracked tractors, 1 gun of 57 (?), 1 howitzer of 105. **6.** 1 tracked vehicle, 1 gun. **7.** 1 semi-tracked tractor, 2 guns, 2 light cars, 1 truck. **8.** 2 trucks, 4 horses. **9.** 1 truck, 1 gun of 105. **10.** 1 light machine gun. **11.** 2 trolleys, 1 truck, 1 cannon, 1 ammunition trailer. **12.** 2 mortars. The casualty record continues beyond this map to No. '31', including 40 horses killed, a third 105-gun, a staff vehicle, three trucks, a light armoured vehicle, and so on. At point '31' the road is impassable. (Heimdal map from a US Army map, with information taken from the maps of Jean Barros)

Sunday, 18 June

Carnage at the hamlet of Jacquin

The day before, 1/39 (a battalion from 9th Division), under the command of Lieutenant Colonel Tucker, had taken a position north of Saint-Jacques-de-Néhou. It was tactically attached to the 60th Infantry Regiment, but had been

West of the hamlet of Jacquin, looking towards the south. The picture is taken from the small road, at the time a track, coming from the north, which was where the Germans arrived from. (GB)

placed in reserve after the capture of Orglandes and was unassigned behind the 60th IR. At 02:00 it was in position on either side of the road leading north from the village, the D87, to the hamlet of Jacquin. The battalion's flanks, however, remain unprotected, and at 04:30, when it was still dark, the GIs heard continuous sub-machine gun and machine gun fire along the 1/39's front lines. Immediately, infantrymen from companies A and B blindly responded from their bivouacs.

A German column from Grenadier-Regiment 1049 arrived from the Bricquebec sector, to the north, heading to the west of Jacquin by a small road at the top of a bend. It was preceded by two armoured vehicles which cleared the road, ahead of the column that consisted of horse-drawn vehicles and bicycle infantrymen. After first being surprised and suffering casualties, the American soldiers reorganised themselves, and the two tanks were destroyed by bazookas. The 1/39's machine-guns and mortars began firing at random. But the Germans approached throwing grenades. The GIs fired 900 rounds, sometimes from 250 metres. Major Ruppenthal notes that a gunner suddenly saw a herd of cows blocking his sight. A sergeant from A Company attempted to scare them off the line of sight by throwing stones and shrapnel at them, but to no effect. He then said to the shooter: 'Never mind, Mike, cut them down with your gun!' But facing the German advance, the 1/60's situation was difficult. At Saint-Jacques-de-Néhou, the 60th Field Artillery Battalion feared a German breakthrough on the right, and so Lieutenant Colonel Tucker ordered the 1/60 to withdraw 400 metres south, on the east-west road crossing Saint-Jacques-de-Néhou, and the men pulled back under the protection of heavy artillery. In their fallback position, Tucker contacted General Eddy by telephone. Eddy approved the retreat but ordered Tucker to hold this new line, with the division's artillery providing support for his battalion. At 09:00, 81 mm mortars began firing constantly on the Germans, who were pushed north to the Scye, where they were also attacked from the air.

During the attack, 1/39 lost thirty-nine men (thirteen killed and twenty-four wounded) and another four or five in the counter-attack. The Germans would leave behind 250 killed and 60 wounded, who were taken prisoner. These were heavy losses for the Germans, a total of 310 men, or about a third of the battalion's strength (and not a full regiment as has been suggested). During these fights of unusual intensity, the inhabitants of Jacquin barricaded themselves in their houses, terrorised for many hours.

And so as the official authorisation for the withdrawal had been granted on 17 June, the Germans from *Kampfgruppe* Hellmich were now trying to retreat south by all available roads during the night of 17-18 June, while at the same time, the Americans had just reached the west coast. Other attempted breakthroughs included several vehicles and a tractor-driven artillery gun trying to cross the Scye at Pont Saint-Paul at 05:00, but a roadblock had been set up to the south of the bridge by 2/60, who had positioned themselves in the Valdecie area three hours earlier, around 02:00, to block the D50 road from Bricquebec and to Portbail.

In the final push to the sea, the 9th Infantry Division was at the forefront. Seen here are two men from one of the division's regiments, the 39th IR, loading a mortar. They are recognisable by the stencilled letters on their headphones: AAAO (Anytime, Anything, Anywhere, Nothing). It was one of the battalions of this regiment, the 1st, who was involved in the terrible fighting at Jacquin before dawn on 18 June. (N/A)

The Pont-Saint-Paul bridge over the Scye, since rebuilt, which blocked the German withdrawal. The Americans were to the south (left) and the Germans came from the north (right). (E.G./Heimdal.)

The 2/60's anti-tank platoon had been placed there with 57 mm guns, while the lead vehicle in the German column was a tractor pulling a 15.2 cm gun. The crews of the 57 mm anti-tank guns opened fire, wounding or killing the German gunmen, and forcing the team into the ditch. The lead vehicles in the column came under fire from the anti-tank guns. Several vehicles were destroyed, while others were captured, and two staff officers were taken prisoner. The rest of the column had to retreat. A German prisoner said that these attempts to break through were carried out by a part of 2nd Battalion and by the 3rd Battalion of Grenadier-Regiment 1049, 77. Infanterie-Division. This division was indeed the furthest from the three divisions who were retreating from the Valognes sector, where it had arrived on 10 June. The other two divisions, including the westernmost 243. Infanterie-Division, had dropped off faster, and its leader, Generallutnant Hellmich, had been killed to the south the day before, near Canville-la-Roque, as he directed the retreat of his units which would later be found at la Haye-du-Puits, as well as part of the 91. Infanterie-Division. The trap had only gradually closed over these divisions. The situation was thus more dramatic for the 77. Infanterie-Division, especially as its leader, General Stegmann had been killed the day before, causing minor panic in the command. Colonel Rudolf Bacherer, the oldest ranking officer, who commanded the Grenadier-Regiment 1049, succeeded General Stegmann at the head of the 77. Infanterie-Division, where he remained. He was an exceptional leader and capable of taking the necessary measures in these dramatic times. In *Invasion! They're Coming*!, Paul Carell wrote down Bacherer's testimony. He held a war council with the principal commanders on 17 June, around 18:00, after the

Born on 9 February 1895 in Pforzheim, Baden Wutenberg, Colonel Rudolf Bacherer saw action in the First World War as an officer in the Baden Dragons Regiment from 13 July 1914 to 1 January 1919. During the Second World War, he participated in the French Campaign and the Russian Campaign from 1941 to 1943. In the West, with the rank of Oberst (colonel), he commanded Grenadier-Regiment 1049, which he succeeded in forcing southwards. In the Haye-du-Puits sector, he commanded the remains of the division under the name of KG 77 ID, or KG Bacherer and would try to stop the Americans on 31 July at Pontaubault. He managed to fall back to Dinard (his unit had been previously garrisoned in this area), where he and his men would resist for ten more days, only surrendering on 15 August 1944. He died on 9 July 1964.

announcement of General Stegmann's death. Bacherer then asked the principal officers for their opinion. Some wanted to give up, others wanted to retreat north under the protection of the guns at Cherbourg. Bacherer objected to this saying it was unreasonable to send thousands of men into captivity, whereas in the south, 'to build the line of resistance, the inclusion of the smallest rifle is vital.'

Another attempt to break the 77. Infanterie-Division took place on the Bricquebec-Barneville road (the D903) on the morning of 18 June. It was carried out by infantry units from 9th Division, the 1/60 and 2/60, and the 60th Field Artillery Battalion's artillery. But, according to the testimony of Charles Montrieul, son of the mayor of Vretot at the time, it was the air force that crushed this German column:

The column was there at 09:30 on Sunday morning, and a wave of planes came over and strafed the road every two minutes in one direction, and every two minutes in the other. They were less than 50 metres over the road. An incendiary bullet was fired every five bullets. You could hear the cases falling on the roof but there was not a single hole made. They were skilled (...) We had taken refuge in the cellar, my father had made a shelter using standing barrels, with large ladders on the top of the barrels, and the granary was filled with hay. (...) 50 metres to the right, four horses were killed, their four heads were together and a young German remained astride his horse, having been killed by a bullet. Between here and the top of the village (Le Vrétot), which is over 250 metres, fifteen horses had been killed... In the afternoon, my father went to see what had happened: in an apple orchard close by, he saw caissons left by the Germans. He lifted the lids, looked inside and found maps showing all the defensive positions at Cherbourg. He handed them over to the first American he saw the next morning (19 June), which allowed the Americans to rethink their plans. (The full testimony appears in n° 41, June 2004, of the *Voix du Donjon*, 50 Bricquebec).

The carnage would continue on this road several kilometres west of Vrétot (see 'E' on the map). But other roads would be used further north ('D'). As Jean Barros notes, two Feldgendarmes who were positioned to regulate the traffic were captured on that day south of the Valdécie.

And so although the cutting off of the peninsula had been effective the day before, it was now reinforced. On that day, in the 60th IR's area of operation in the north, Barneville had been the objective for 3/60. At 22:00 on 17 June, C Company, in the lead, climbed on five tanks, four tank-destroyers, and the four half-tracks belonging to the anti-tank platoon, and set off from the crossroads located north of the Valdécie, reaching the Croix aux Pelletiers crossroads before proceeding along the D42. Around 3 kilometres from their starting point, the column came across a German anti-tank gun. The march resumed again after the skirmish, but at the crossroads north of Saint-Maurice, the Americans took the wrong road, continuing straight up to the hamlet of Villot, arriving there at 02:00 on 18 June, just missing a German cyclist column that was retreating south. The 3/60 then veered right on the main road and reached Barneville in the east, arriving near the water tower, at the highest point overlooking the sea. The peninsula was officially cut off and there is now a memorial here to commemorate the event.

This aerial photograph shows Barneville looking east, from where the American soldiers arrived. The plane is flying from the direction of the sea, which is behind the photographer. The village stretches along the coastal road linking les Pieux to the north and la Haye-du-Puits to the south. (DF/Heimdal)

18 June 2004: a ceremony marking the 60th anniversary of the cutting of the Cotentin Peninsula in Barneville. The memorial, which stands to the south of the locality, was erected at the place where the 9th Division reached the sea. (J. Bavay)

The 3/60 settled on this high ground and sent its K Company into Barneville, accompanied by armoured vehicles. The peninsula had been cut off while the German columns were still in retreat. This meant that at 10:00, about 125 Germans attacked to the south-east; L Company counter-attacked and 85 of them were captured (see photos). The Battle of the Cotentin Peninsula ended here, but the battle for Cherbourg would now begin and the units would soon be redeployed to the north.

Montebourg: Keil withdraws

On 18 June, thanks to the US breakthrough in the west, the situation became even more critical for *Kamfgruppe* Keil. The light-armoured Panzer-Ersatz-Abteilung 101 was ordered to leave Montebourg on the night of 18-19 June and head for Valognes,a small town at the heart of the Cotentin Peninsula. Its origins go back to Roman times, although it had enjoyed a certain fame in the classical period. It was called the 'little Normandy Versailles' due to its many private mansions occupied by the local aristocracy. But Valognes is also an important road crux in the centre of the peninsula, meaning it was now the next obstacle on the RN13 road between Montebourg and Cherbourg. Finally, the open breach on the right of *Unterkampfgruppe* Hoffmann directly threatened Valognes. This meant that to the west of Montebourg, there was no longer any German front line. Valognes was directly threatened and Montebourg could now be bypassed by the rear. Unfortunately, the Americans had not realised this and continued to attack Montebourg, which still held, despite the preparations for the withdrawal. Further east, Lieutenant Colonel Müller was still at his CP at Hill 45, near Octeville-l'Avenel (this CP was also bombed on 16 and 17 June), and he held firmly onto his line to the north of the Sinope.

Barneville, 18 June 1944

At Barneville, on the morning of 18 June, Constable Fourneau and another gendarme captured two Germans and handed them over to the Americans. French civilians would often participate, sometimes involuntarily, in the discovery of small groups of isolated German soldiers. As Jean Barros notes, 'At Monsieur Aimable Baumel's farm, situated on the chemin des Courtes, his son René discovered nine German soldiers who had taken refuge in the stable, and succeeded in persuading them to surrender.' In this picture, the two gendarmes are seen handing over the two German prisoners to the Americans, in front of the Hotel de Paris. (J. Barros)

Carrying the wounded in Barneville, 18 June. The man with the cap on the left, near the German prisoner, is Monsieur Van Den Brouck. (N/A)

The German prisoners are gathered together in the church square. As Jean Barros notes, 'For these prisoners, the war was over, others did not have that chance. On the morning of 18 June, two German soldiers were killed by the Americans. One, aged 19, was killed on the rue Hauvet, and the other near the town hall.' (N/A)

In Barneville, small groups of isolated Germans were also taken prisoner by American soldiers. For them, the war was over. They are almost all (except for the second on the left) wearing the standard issue cap, the Einheitsfeldmütze. (N/A)

1 & 2. *'The liberation involves very moving memories. I saw the first American soldier seated on our neighbours' doorstep, Monsieur and Madame Legendre (now a doctor's surgery). We had just been told by Monsieur Guillemet who had courageously gone out to see what was happening and came back shouting: "You can come out, the Americans are here!" There were a lot of people out there. I mostly remember a parade of military trucks, so we went to pick all the roses from the garden and threw them on the tanks.'* Testimony of Madame Buhot, reported by Jean Barros. Doctor Jean Auvret is seen here shaking hands with an American soldier, in front of what was the town hall at the time. (N/A)

3 & 4. These American photographs were taken on 19 June, in Carteret. The captions read: 'The civilians in Carteret rush to welcome the first American soldiers arriving in their city. Bouquets of flowers and wine are offered and the children are picked up so that they can see their American liberators.' These photographs were incorrectly dated as 23 June by the Americans. (N/A)

Carteret, 19 June

1. Aerial photograph of Bricquebec, surrounding its medieval castle, looking north.

2. This other photograph is taken looking the south, with the chateau des Galleries in the foreground.

1. Near Bricquebec, medics from the 39th RI, 9th Infantry Division, give a glass of wine to a German soldier who has been wounded in the neck. It must be a soldier from 77. ID, who had come under fire from the American 60th Field Artillery Battalion, on the road from Barneville to Bricquebec. On the helmet of one of the medics can be seen a stencil inscription peculiar to this particular regiment: AAAO, which stands for Anytime, Anything, Anywhere, Nothing.

2. Place des Buttes in Bricquebec, dominated by the keep of the medieval castle. Overlooking the square is the J. Feuardent coffee shop and the cider-coffee shop, *Au Soleil Levant*, belonging to A. Touquet.

1 & 2. Two GIs pass in front of Monsieur Durel's butcher's shop on 22 June. Although there was no longer any German opposition, the Rue Saint-Roch (seen here), near the bridge, was the only place that was bombed. The houses located there were rebuilt.

3. The same square today. The restaurant is still there, but it now has a covered terrace.

4. This modern photograph shows the area around the bridge that was destroyed. Looking south-east, the castle can be seen in the background. (NA/EG/Heimdal)

5

North, to Cherbourg

Monday, 19 June

Now that the Contentin Peninsula was taken, with the four German divisions cut in two and reduced to nothing but tactical groups retreating to 'Festung Cherbourg' (Fortress Cherbourg), the Americans had a strong numerical superiority with which to launch their offensive on the city. They had four infantry divisions (from west to east): the 9th Infantry Division (General Eddy), the 90th Infantry Division (General Landrum), the 79th Infantry Division (General Wyche) and the 4th Infantry Division (General Barton). The availability of resources meant that it was possible to remove the 90th which was of no great surprise. The 9th Infantry Division, which has completed the breakthrough to the sea, would attack along the west coast, towards La Hague, supported by the 4th Cavalry Group. Along the east coast, opposite Quinéville and Montebourg, the 4th Infantry Division would continue to fulfil the mission it had been given on 6 June, while the 79th Infantry Division would attack in the centre, towards Valognes and Cherbourg.

Opposite the 9th Infantry Division were the Germans elements of Infaterie-Regiments 920 and 921 (243. Infanterie-Division) as well as elements from Infaterie-Regiments 1049 and 1050 (77. Infaterie-Division). Facing the 79th Infantry Division, between the Douve and the Merderet, were the other elements from Infaterie-Regiment 1049 and elements of Infaterie-Regiment 1057 (91. LuftLande). Finally, the 4th Infantry Division was primarily up against *Kampfgruppe* Keil and *Kampfgruppe* Müller.

The attack on 19 June began at 05:00. The 9th Infantry Division's objectives were Saint-Germain-le-Gaillard and Rauville-la-Bigot. The 79th Infantry Division had to seize the high ground to the west and north-west of Valognes, but the final objective was, of course, Cherbourg.

In the Montebourg sector, the 4th Infantry Division prepared for the final assault. General Barton ordered the 8th Infantry Regiment to the west of the railway line and the 12th Infantry Regiment east of the railway. The attack began at 03:00, without any artillery preparation, and with the two regiments having to skirt around the area. If necessary, the 183rd Field Artillery Battalion's 155 mm howitzers and the tank destroyers from the 801st Battalion would intervene. As we have seen, the American front now comprised of a salient east of Montebourg. It was a favourable position for the 12th Infantry Regiment, which was ordered to take Hills 100 and 119 that dominated the entire area, north of Montebourg. Despite initially coming under fire from German artillery and rocket launchers, the regiment advanced anyway and at 10:00, Hoffmann reported to Keil that the American attack was progressing and that 'American armoured vehicles were approaching the high ground north of Montebourg'. The 12th Infantry Regiment's 2nd Battalion took Hill 100 but further to the east, the 3rd Battalion stopped advancing as it had to wait for the tanks that were currently supporting 1st

Battalion. It would not be able to take Hill 119 until around 16:00, when it finally received the tank support it needed.

To the west, Colonel Van Fleet's 8th Infantry Regiment would have more difficulties as the German grenadiers had dug their foxholes along the Montebourg-Le Ham railway. At 02:50, in the rain, Captain John A. Kulp understood that if the weather did not change, then they would not be able to rely on any tactical aviation support. Along with his men from F Company, 2nd Battalion (2/8), he left the main road and had ten minutes to get back to his starting position. Preceded by a mortar attack by Colonel Van Fleet, he tried to keep behind the exploding shells as much as possible, even though the heat of the explosions burned his face. During the night, he passed through the German front line and, without any major contact, reached his objective 900 metres north-west of Montebourg. However, he had only forty-five men around him, as two-thirds of his company had stayed behind. Lieutenant John C. Rebarchek, the commander of E company, was making his way down a sunken road when he found himself face to face with the men of one of Kulp's sections, which had been trapped by the fighting, and he went on to join Kulp in his position. In general, the fighting throughout this area where the Germans had dug in among the *bocage* was fierce, and would require tank support in order succeed.

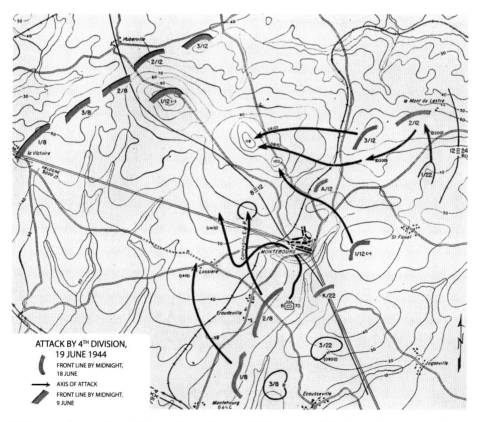

Following the attack on 19 June, Kampfgruppe Keil evacuated the Montebourg sector in an organised manner on the night of 19-20 June. (US Army map)

At noon, the Germans were ordered to withdraw back to the Valognes-Quettehou road and hold this new line of resistance until 23:00. The wet weather made it easier for this general withdrawal to Festung Cherbourg and was done without the knowledge of the Americans. However, some clashes did take place and Keil was momentarily cut off from the rearguards of I./922. In the evening, the front line was reconstructed along the Valognes-Quettehou road with the Georgian battalion, the I./922, and the II./729, after the commander of unit was wounded. There was still no contact with the Americans, but contact was maintained with *Kampfgruppe* Müller.

However, this withdrawal was just a first step and the retreat resumed, as expected, from 23:00. Keil took the following route: Saint-Martin d'Audouville, Saint-Germain-de-Tournebu, Montaigu-la-Brisette, Saussemesnil, Mesnil-au-Val, La Glacerie, Cherbourg, noting in his written report for the Americans after he'd been captured: 'After the Americans broke through on 17 June, it was clear to every man that our positions were now lost. However, morale remained good. The men who had no experience of combat became real soldiers following two weeks of hard fighting, and felt morally superior to the enemy.'

In his book, *Utah Beach to Cherbourg*, Major Roland G. Ruppenthal writes that in the afternoon the German resistance around Montebourg stopped and

A small monument dedicated 'to widows and orphans' in the cemetery of Saint-Pierre-d'Arthéglise - a rare tribute to the civilian victims of the battle. (J. Bavay)

the retreat began. In fact, until around noon, the Germans had continued to resist the American assault on their positions. After this, they follow the orders to withdraw and pulled back in good order. Sporadic fighting still took place, but this was due to clashes with elements of the rearguard as they fell back. A section from I./922 and II./920 remained in their positions until dawn on 20 June in order to deceive the Americans as to the exact situation. In spite of some skirmishes with retreating elements, the Americans now had nothing in front of them, and were easily able to seize Montebourg and all the area located to the north. Two weeks after the invasion and after ten days of hard fighting, the cornerstone of the German front before Cherbourg, Montebourg, was finally in the hands of the Americans.

The Germans methodically followed the orders for a general withdrawal on Festung Cherbourg. The 9th Infantry Division and the 79th Infantry Division would advance rapidly as the Germans retreated before them, with the two divisions only delayed by obstacles caused by the Engineering units or elements left behind in order to slow down their progress. The 9th Infantry Division even managed to advance 16 kilometres, arrivingat Pious in the evening. Meanwhile, the 79th Infantry Division had managed to reach Valognes. Once again, it was in the Montebourg sector where the advance was the weakest, but now it was time for the Battle of Cherbourg to begin.

Bricquebec sector after the battle

German prisoners in Place des Buttes, Bricquebec. (La Voix du Donjon)

1. Ceremony at Bricquebec cemetery in July 1944, with the Mayor (Marcel Grillard), schoolchildren, the Americans and a British officer. (La Voix du Donjon)

2. Lieutenant James L. Larkin, a glider officer, fell in the middle of the German lines on 6 June and hid until the Americans arrived.

3. Around noon on 11 June, Ralph Smathers' P-47 plane was shot down by Flak over Rocheville (east of Bricquebec). He hid in a small house and the young Ginette Simon (now Madame Lahaye), aged sixteen, served as an interpreter. The pilot had burns on his neck and legs and was taken away in an ambulance eight days later when the Americans arrived. He is seen here when he returned on 14 August 1944, to thank the inhabitants of Rocheville. (G. Lahaye)

4. April 2003 (L to R): The Mayor of Rocheville, André Fratissier; Ralph Smathers; Simon Fratissier; Ginette Lahaye.

Montebourg, 17-20 June

1. This photo was taken south of Montebourg, near the front line which would stay in place until the morning of 19 June. An American vehicle has tipped over after being hit by a German shell. The *Kampfgruppe* of Lieutenant Colonel Keil (III./919) kept a firm hold of this cornerstone of the German front. However, the Americans pushed through westward to Carteret on 17 June, and from there went north towards Cherbourg. The Germans were thus forced to retreat and abandon Montebourg. The dominant, strategic position of the locality can be appreciated here. (D.F/E.G./Heimdal)

2 & 3. By 20 June, American troops were in Montebourg which had been evacuated. Seen here are jeeps belonging to the 4th Infantry Division.

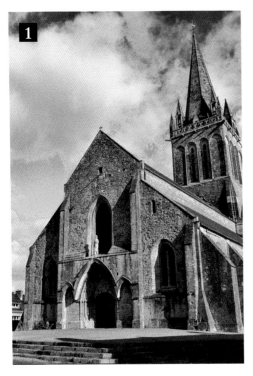

1. The beautiful, Medieval church in Montebourg dominates the area. (D.F/E.G./Heimdal)

2. This aerial photograph, looking east towards the coast (Cherbourg is to the left and Sainte-Mère-Eglise to the right), shows the extent of the destruction in Montebourg, which was ravaged by Allied naval artillery on 11 June. The central square, where the market stood, can be seen, as well as another smaller square dominated by the massive silhouette of the church.

Montebourg, 20 June

On 18 June, KG Keil was ordered to leave Montebourg on the night of 18-19 June and to retreat to Valognes. The town had been the cornerstone of the German resistance in front of Cherbourg for a dozen days.

3. US troops entered the locality on 19 June after the German withdrawal. This picture was taken on 20 June, on the main road from Carentan that heads north towards Valognes, at the entrance to the central square. A civilian attempts to pass near a destroyed vehicle: nearly 300 civilians survived among the ruins.

4 & 5. In this picture, the war correspondent Franklin has walked a few metres down the road and turned to take a new photograph looking south. The destroyed vehicle from the previous picture can still be seen. The destroyed buildings on the left were re-built further back from the road.

1 & 2. Continuing along the square presents a scene of desolation, including some wandering goats. (NA./E.G./Heimdal)

3. The walls of the church are still marked by impacts.

4 & 5. From a distance, the bell tower of Montebourg church dominates the whole region. It was hit by shelling in June 1944, but the damaged church held firm.

1. The interior of the church on 21 June.

2. A child repairs a bicycle near a destroyed vehicle on 23 June.

3. War correspondent Collier wrote 'saved for the toast' to evoke the unusual fate of these fragile glasses, preserved in a destroyed house in Montebourg on 28 June. (6053)

4 & 5. 'Requisitioned'. On 21 June, the American infantry uses carts and horses from the German Army to transport supplies. The photograph was taken in front of No. 40 (currently No. 32) on rue Verblay, which had remained intact. However, further down the road, numbers 5 to 18 had to be rebuilt. (5686)

1 & 2. Further ahead, a new house has replaced the ruins. (D.F./E.G./Heimdal)

3. The fires were terrible and the houses are seen still smoking.

4. In Place A. Pélerin, the *Hotel Restaurant du Midi* has been rebuilt. In this square, No.s 12, 14, 16, 18, 20 and 22 survived without much damage.

Montebourg, 20 June

1 & 2. The *Hotel du Midi* in 1944 and today.

3. The statue was moved from the square to a new position.

4. Horses were used for transportation. These GIs are using a German horse-drawn cart to bring water and supplies to their colleagues on the front line.

1. Another view of the square, this time showing a jeep.

2. A convoy, en route to the front, travels through the ruins.

3 & 4. Memorial monuments. (D.F./E.G./ Heimdal)

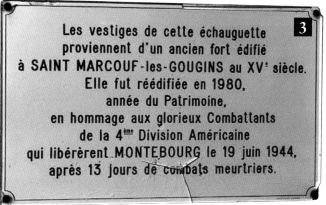

Les vestiges de cette échauguette proviennent d'un ancien fort édifié à SAINT MARCOUF-les-GOUGINS au XVᵉ siècle. Elle fut réédifiée en 1980, année du Patrimoine, en hommage aux glorieux Combattants de la 4ᵉᵐᵉ Division Américaine qui libérèrent MONTEBOURG le 19 juin 1944, après 13 jours de combats meurtriers.

Portbail

These remarkable, unpublished photographs, showing Portbail, Barneville and Saint-Lô d'Ourville, are from two albums belonging to Corporal Perrel E. Harford, who worked in the laundry of an American field hospital, 200th QM Laundry (Hosp.). Having left England on 17 July 1944, he eventually reached Bolleville on 3 December and was attached to the 174th General Hospital until May 1945. Although taken eight months after the fighting, his photos remain an exceptional account of the area after the battle.

1 & 2. At the time, a small railway line ran from Carentan to the seaside resort of Carteret. Corporal Harford is photographed here in front of Portbail station, which still exists, although parts of the line have been taken out of service.

1&2. Destruction in the central square of Portbail, north of Saint-Martin's church, rue Hellouin. The ruins were replaced by new buildings after the war.

3. Harford is seen now in the centre of Portbail, in front of the post office located to the south of Saint-Martin's church. The church itself was damaged, but the post office remained intact.

PORT-BAIL

LEGRAPHE   POSTE   TELEPHONE

1. Other damaged buildings.

2 & 3. The Czech hedgehogs used to prevent tanks from landing are still in place. (Photographs: Harford/Heimdal. Current photographs: Erik Groult/Heimdal)

Portbail

On 19 June, the town of Portbail was the victim of artillery duels between the Americans and Germans. An American battery was positioned at La Picauderie (crossroads of the D903 and the D50 on the coastal road from Bricquebec to Portbail). Another battery was positioned at Mont de Besneville. Meanwhile, the Germans had set up a battery at Mont-de-Doville (high ground south of the 'marsh line'), and batteries in the Denneville sector. Consequently, Portbail suffered from American fire from La Picauderie (north-east) and German fire from the south-east. According to several testimonies collected by Jean Barros, Portbail burned for almost a week, despite the intervention of volunteers and courageous rescuers, 'but without effective means to fight fires'. The fires were further fuelled by the equinox storm. As well as causing casualties, the artillery fire completely destroyed forty-five buildings, while another ninety were partially damaged, as well as Saint-Martin's church.

1&2. The burned-down Saint-Martin's church, in the centre of town, and now.

1. The devastated choir. The window above the altar would be blocked-up during the restoration, as can be seen in the next picture, as well as the two doors leading to the sacristy.

2. The restored nave and the southern aisle, on the right, beyond the great fifteenth-century arcades. The church is Medieval, presenting parts stretching from the Romanesque period until the end of the fifteenth century.

3 & 4. The northern chapel, at the beginning of 1945 and now restored.

5. Detail of the chapel's arch showing traces of the fire that gnawed away at the stone.

6 & 7. The other church, Notre-Dame, with its fortified bell tower, dominates the harbour in front of the sea. (Photographs: Corporal Harford (Heimdal). Photographs 2, 4, 6, 7 and 9: Erik Groult/Heimdal)

Barneville

1 & 2. The water tower dominates the village of Barneville at its highest point, above the church. Its Medieval castle pastiche attracted the attention of Corporal Harford.

3 & 4. Barneville Station. The railway line on this stretch is still in use as a small tourist train.

5 & 6. Photographs showing Barneville beach. The damaged seaside villa on the right has been razed. On the other hand, the house with the four-sided roof (centre) still stands.

A comrade of Corporal Harford poses on the coastal road, probably at the crossroads with the D50.

A villa since destroyed.

1 & 2. The beach was dotted with Czech hedgehogs. The coast had also been reinforced by German resistance nests, but these were less frequent and less powerful than on the east coast. The area was less accessible to the Allies, but was under threat from the artillery batteries on the Channel Islands. (Photos: Corporal Harford/Heimdal. Current photographs: E.Groult/Heimdal)

Saint-Lô d'Ourville

1&2. American soldiers photographed in front of the cafe. Corporal Harford, impeccably dressed, is second from the right.

1,2, & 3. The entrance east of the village (Portbail and the sea are straight ahead, at the end of this road). Corporal Harford is seen in Image 2, posing at the village entrance, which was still defended by concrete walls built by the Germans. The site is currently intact, only the concrete walls have disappeared. The cafe is on the right.

This photograph was taken at the entrance of Saint-Lô d'Ourville by Corporal Harford in early 1945. (Heimdal and E.G./Heimdal for the two current photographs)

Saint-Lô d'Ourville, Carcan Bridge

Here we see Corporal Harford photographed in the opposite direction, looking north, and the Saint-Lô d'Ourville/Portbail road. You can see the sides of the concrete walls, which have since disappeared.

1

2

1, 2 & 3. Two photographs by Corporal Harford, and a current photograph taken at the same location, showing access to the Carcan Bridge, looking south. This is how Colonel Bacherer was able to break through with his men on 19 June 1944. The front would remain blocked here until 2 July, with the Germans holding the south shore of the Grise, which can be seen opposite. It should be noted that before the invasion, the Germans had erected a concrete wall with a firing point at this strategic point, south of the road linking Saint-Lô d'Ourville to Portbail. These photographs by Corporal Harford, taken eight months later, are also valuable documents. (Harford, Heimdal, and current photograph, E.G./Heimdal)

4. Photograph of Corporal Harford taken on the D50 (then the GC50) near the crossroads with the D903, where Colonel Bacherer passed. (Harford/Heimdal)

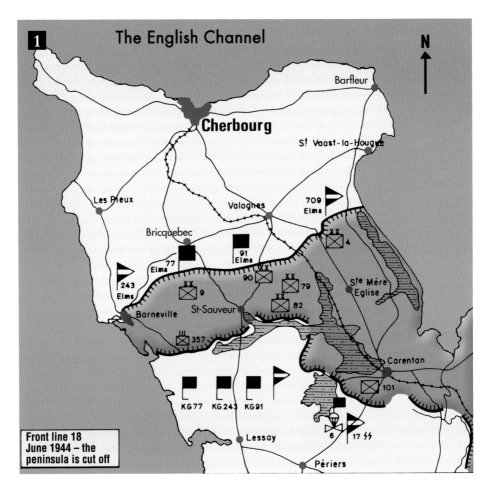

1. This map shows the front line by the evening of 18 June 1944. The 9th Infantry Division cut the Cotentin Peninsula after reaching Barneville. Elements of four German divisions (243rd, 77th, 91st and 709th) were now isolated, encircled to the north. Other elements from these divisions managed to retreat south and escape being surrounded. After the withdrawal of the 90th and the rest of the 82nd to the south, three US divisions (9th, 79th and 4th) now advanced towards Cherbourg to face the Germans who were retreating to the *Festung*. (Heimdal)

2. Colonel Bacherer's epic route on 19 June. (Jean Barros).

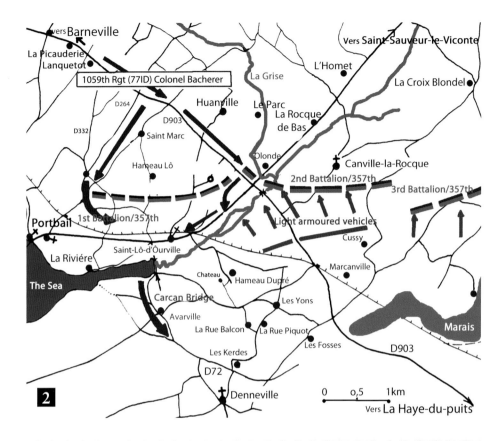

Colonel Bacherer's Odyssey

After the dramatic breakthrough attempts of the 77. Infanterie-Division
(see chapter 4), Colonel Bacherer embraced the new situation energetically.
Losses numbering a few hundred were sustained at the three crossing points
at dawn on 18 June, but this was in a division that comprised of 10,505 men
(with the Hiwis) in early June. Colonel Bacherer now had to wait until the next
night and the darkness to pass. On 19 June, he assembled about 1,500 men
and at 01:00, the column set out. Doctor Schreihage, a staff officer, described
the journey: several Kübelwagen (Volkswagens), including two radio vehicles,
were at the front and informed the units at the back of the units' progress. The
column reached the Villot hamlet (see map on page x) and Bacherer conveyed
the following order: 'Push on to Villot!' Then, as dawn approached, they
reached 'Olonde Creek' (which was actually the Grise River, near the manor of
Olonde), and at around 11:00, under a cloudy sky, landed right in the middle
of the American 2/357th Infantry Regiment. Using two assault guns from the
243.Infanterie-Division, Colonel Bacherer attacked 'in the old manner' with the
I./1050 advancing with fixed bayonets, supported by light machine-gun fire. In
total, 1,400 German soldiers attacked and captured 250 American prisoners
(although American historians put the figure nearer to 100) with 12 jeeps!

Further information

This battlefield is rich with sites to discover. To the north, Montebourg was bruised by the fighting and one can use the comparative photographs to explore this 'cornerstone' of the front. One can also visit the Azeville and Crisbecq batteries which are nearby. Further on is La Pernelle, where Colonel Triepel's CP and Lieutenant Colonel Keil's CP were located before the battle, with beautiful views towards Utah Beach.

To the west are the sites of La Fière, before continuing on to Cauquigny then Amfreville (see Chapter 1 and Chapter 3). The German military cemetery is located at Orglandes and includes the burial sites of three generals. The dramatic route taken on 17 June between Saint-Jacques-de-Néhou and Bricquebec is there to be explored, including the hamlet of Jacquin (and the nearby Camp Patton), as well as the crossroads of Vente au Saulniers and Pont Saint-Paul. The Malassis residence nearby is private property, but you can reach the entrance via the narrow road, from where you can see the chateau, opposite, and the manor, below. Saint-Sauveur-le-Vicomte, where the bridge over the Douve is dominated by the magnificent castle, is a reminder that this place was as essential to the breakthrough as the Chaussée de la Fière. In Sortosville, you can visit the Luftwaffe's radio-guidance bunker that overlooks the area towards Barneville. Finally, Carteret and Barneville, in particular, remind us of the ultimate objective of the breakthrough. In Portbail and especially at Saint-Lô-d'Ourville, at the Carcan Bridge, you can discover traces of Colonel Bacherer's epic odyssey.

Bibliography

Ruppenthal, Major Roland G., *Utah Beach to Cherbourg* (Historical Division Department of the Army, USA, 1947)

An important, accurate work describing US military operations. Its rich iconography cannot be discounted.

Barros, Jean, *1944-1945, La côte des Isles dans la tourmente des combats pour la libération et la coupure du Cotentin*

A very rich document describing the fighting in the Barneville-Carteret canton, which details the German positions of the Atlantic Wall and the battles of the 9th Division and the cutting of the peninsula. It also includes very accurate maps of this area. Recommended. Available from the Tourist Office, 50270 Barneville-Carteret.

Hamel, André, *Six ans de guerre 1939-1945, la 9th Division US d'Utah Beach à Goury* (André Hamel, Les Pieux, 1994)

Keil, Günther, *Memoir* (Records National Archives)

A detailed report written in captivity at the request of the Americans. A rare document that shows the German side of the story, it is essential reading for information on the fighting in the area around Montebourg.

Carrell, Paul, *Invasion! They're Coming!* (Dutton, New York, 1963)

Konrad von Keusgen, Helmut, *Die Kanonenvon Saint Marcouf* (HEK Verlag, Garbsen, 2005)

A very detailed and richly illustrated book concerning the two batteries at Azeville and Crisbecq. Essential reading.